Boys' performance in Modern Foreign Languages

Centre for Information
on Language Teaching and Research

The Centre for Information on Language Teaching and Research provides a complete range of services for language professionals in every stage and sector of education, and in business, in support of its brief to promote Britain's foreign language capability.

CILT is a registered charity, supported by Central Government grants. CILT is based in Covent Garden, London, and its services are delivered through a national collaborative network of regional Comenius Centres in England, the National Comenius Centre of Wales, Scottish CILT and Northern Ireland CILT.

CILT Publications are available through all good booksellers or directly from:

Central Books, 99 Wallis Rd,
London E9 5LN.
Tel: 020 8986 4854. Fax: 020 8533 5821.

boys'
performance
in modern foreign languages

listening to learners

A project carried out
by Homerton College, Cambridge
on behalf of QCA

Barry Jones
Gwenneth Jones

WITH CONTRIBUTIONS BY:
Helen Demetriou
Peter Downes
Jean Rudduck

HOMERTON COLLEGE
CAMBRIDGE

The views expressed in this publication are the authors' and do not necessarily represent those of CILT.

Acknowledgements

The authors and research team would like to thank in particular Tim Oates and Pat Tunstall from QCA for their consistent and helpful support; LEA advisers for their promptness in identifying appropriate schools to contact; the Head Teachers, Heads of Department and teachers in the seven schools for their willingness to organise and participate in interviews and consultation; the pupils in Year 9 and Year 11 for their frankness, honesty and good nature during the focus groups and interviews; Marc Padellec and Emma Rees from CILT for their excellent design suggestions and advice prior to publication; and Viv Brans for the many versions she photocopied and bound during the life of the project.

First published 2001 by the Centre for Information on Language Teaching and Research (CILT)
20 Bedfordbury, London WC2N 4LB
Copyright © Centre for Information on Language Teaching and Research 2001

Cover photography © 2000, Barbara Ludman/iwitness

ISBN 1 902031 94 6

2005 2004 2003 2002 2001 / 10 9 8 7 6 5 4 3 2 1

A catalogue record for this book is available from the British Library

Printed in Great Britain by Copyprint UK Ltd

CILT Publications are available from: **Central Books,** 99 Wallis Rd, London E9 5LN. Tel: 020 8986 4854. Fax: 020 8533 5821. Book trade representation (UK and Ireland): **Broadcast Book Services,** Charter House, 27a London Road, Croydon CR0 2RE. Tel: 020 8681 8949. Fax: 020 8688 0615.

Contents

Note: the referencing system used in the report

All quotations shown in this report have been chosen as representative of views expressed by the pupils in Years 9 and 11. Sometimes, therefore, a comment from a pupil in Year 9 has been included rather than one from Year 11, or vice versa, because it is a more articulate or telling summary of one particular opinion. Because, however, the research is qualitative rather than quantitative, no systematic attempt has been made to record the frequency within the data with which comments occur.

All comments are quoted verbatim. Omissions from actual words used are marked like this (...) and have been made only to avoid repetition and to ensure clarity. They have not otherwise been edited.

Codes used refer to individual pupils and to particular parts of the data. The final figures after a colon (:9 :11) show the pupil's year group – Year 9 being 13–14 year old pupils, and Year 11 being pupils aged 15–16, in their last year of compulsory secondary schooling who will take the General Certificate of Secondary Education (GCSE) examinations in May/June.

1 Introduction

At the North of England Education Conference in 1998, the then Minister, Stephen Byers, signalled the government's commitment to trying to identify reasons for boys' under-performance and to finding strategies to remedy the situation. Three years later, boys' performance remains a national concern.

A recent review of research on gender and performance undertaken for the Office for Standards in Education (OFSTED) identified two areas where there was clear evidence that boys were performing less well than girls (Arnot et al, 1998). Firstly, girls get off to a better start in literacy skills: the gap is apparent as pupils start school and remains sizeable throughout pupils' primary schooling and into the secondary phase. Secondly, girls have been making greater progress between the ages of 11 and 16 than boys. For example, boys perform less well than girls at GCSE: a gap in the proportions of boys and girls securing five or more higher grade passes began to emerge in the late 1980s and has remained throughout the 1990s. Girls outperform boys quite markedly in English – and although there has been less national publicity for the figures, there is a similar pattern in relation to Modern Foreign Languages.

Finding explanations for the differences between boys' and girls' progress is no easy task. The OFSTED Report identified a range of possible explanations, including patterns of classroom learning established at an early stage in pupils' school careers; gendered patterns of classroom behaviour; the nature of the learning task and of the form of assessment; the extent to which a subject is language-based; gender stereotyping as it affects perceptions of subjects and subject choices; peer group cultures and their definitions of acceptable learning behaviours; and the impact on motivation to learn of loss of traditional manual employment opportunities in local communities.

In relation to Modern Foreign Languages, accounts by teachers suggest that boys' enthusiasm for the subject tends to decline after Years 7 and 8 and that this disaffection is not limited to boys of lower academic aptitude. One outcome is that fewer boys choose to continue with languages for Advanced level (A level); recruitment to university specialist language degrees is also predominantly female; more women than men are recruited to MFL teacher training programmes.

The Qualifications and Curriculum Authority (QCA) decided, in autumn 1998, to support a one-year study of boys' performance and Modern Foreign Languages; the contract was won by a team based at Homerton College, Cambridge, and the overall grant was just under £20,000. The study started in March 1999 and ended in April 2000.

A distinctive feature of the project was its concern to collect data from pupils as well as from their teachers. As Hodgkin has said:

> *The fact is that pupils themselves have a huge potential contribution to make, not as passive objects but as active players in the education system. Any (policy) concerning school standards will be seriously weakened if it fails to recognise the importance of that contribution.* (Hodgkin, 1998, p11)

In the early nineties questions were being asked about the neglect of the pupil perspective (see Rudduck et al, 1996). In the United States, for instance, Erickson and Schultz point out that 'virtually no research has been done that places student experience at the centre of attention' (1992, p476, quoted by Levin, 1995, p17). In Canada, Fullan asked, in relation to school reform: 'what would happen if we treated the student as someone whose opinion mattered …?' (1991, p170). In Sweden, Andersson said that 'politicians who decide about school reforms and the teachers who run the classrooms seldom ask how the students themselves perceive their school' (1995, p5). Levin, from Canada, notes that while the literature on school-based management advocates more important roles for teachers and parents ' … students are usually omitted from the discussion' (1995, p17). And Nieto, from the United States brings the issue of pupil perspective firmly into the school improvement frame when she says,

> *One way to begin the process of changing school policies is to listen to students' views about them; however, research that focuses on student voice is relatively recent and scarce.* (1994, pp395–396)

She points out that pupils' perspectives have, for the most part, 'been missing in discussions concerning strategies for confronting educational problems'.

Patricia Phelan and her colleagues (also from North America) argue that it is important to give attention to students' views of things that affect their learning – not so much factors outside school but those in school that teachers and policy-makers have some power to change (1992, p696). And in the UK we, along with other researchers, have argued that pupils are our expert witnesses in the process of school improvement (Rudduck, 1996).

In the UK, policy-makers are responding positively. The QCA has recently commissioned parallel studies of pupil perspectives on assessment and on the national curriculum; the Department for Education and Employment (DfEE) has emphasised the importance of the pupil perspective in many of the research projects that it is funding. And teachers up and down the country are finding ways of tuning in to pupils' accounts of teaching and learning in school (see Rudduck, 1999, Rudduck et al, 1996).

2 Approach

Introduction: the national pattern

Over the last four years the modern foreign languages results at GCSE have shown a pattern, nationally, where girls are doing considerably better than boys. In 1999, 74% of Year 11 boys and 83% of Year 11 girls took GCSE in Modern Foreign Languages (these are 'combined' – i.e. entries for all languages and including pupils who were entered for more than one language). 47% of the girls entered achieved a higher grade pass and 31% of boys – a gap of 16%; the gap was 15% in 1997 and 16% in 1998. The gap in English in 1999 was also 16%.

2.1 The selection of schools

Within the project we wanted to work with some schools whose results for Modern Foreign Languages reflected the national pattern (the group A schools) and with whom many schools in the system could identify. We also wanted to find other schools which appeared, from their GCSE results, to be 'bucking the trend' (the B/A schools) or to be 'clearly bucking the trend' (the B schools). In identifying the schools we consulted local education authority MFL advisers/inspectors and matched schools against a set of selection criteria.

In addition to performance criteria, where we looked at both residual scores for MFL and GCSE higher grade passes, we used the following five criteria:

- a comprehensive intake, admitting both boys and girls;
- an annual cohort of at least 120 pupils (excluding Years 12 and 13);
- a clear majority of pupils for whom English is the first language;
- a reasonably stable staffing pattern in MFL;
- a languages policy where pupils are setted by ability in Years 9 and 11.

The other two criteria were these:

- a pass rate of GCSE 5+ A* – Cs that was up to 15% higher or lower than the national average and a reasonably stable pattern of results over a three-year period (i.e. we were trying to avoid schools which were strikingly above or strikingly below the national average, or which showed erratic patterns of results);

- a residual score for boys in MFL that was, for the A schools, similar to the national pattern and, for the B/A and B schools, a residual score for boys in MFL that was rather better than the national average.

Residual scores for each subject are available nationally, at local authority level and at school level. At school level, the residual scores show the gap between the performance of the pupils taking a particular subject and the performance of the pupils in the school as a whole. If the residual in a subject is +0.50, that means that the average performance of pupils in that subject is half a grade **higher** than their performance in **all** subjects in that school. If a subject has a negative residual, then the relationship is reversed. Residuals can also show the difference in performance, by subject, between boys and girls in the school.

Nationally, pupils do less well in MFL than they do in other subjects. In 1997 the **national** residual for boys for French was –0.46; in 1998 it was –0.42. The residual for girls was negative but slightly higher than that of boys: –0.14 in 1997 and –0.09 in 1998. (Although the project started in 1999, the national residuals are always a year behind and we had, therefore, to use the 1998 and 1997 data.) Although it was possible to compare the performance of both boys and girls in the same school, our main comparison was between boys' performance in MFL and boys' performance in other subjects in the school; these data gave us a picture of schools where boys seemed to be underperforming in the target subject.

In looking at both residuals and GCSE passes we focused on performance in French. The residuals for German are also negative but boys are doing better in German than they do in French. In terms of GCSE results, 48% of boys entered for GCSE German achieved a higher grade pass and 62% of girls (the comparable figures for French are 43% and 58%). The difference between the two languages is explained by the fact that the minority of more able pupils who take two languages usually take German in addition to French.

The table below shows the residual scores for boys, for French, across the seven schools:

| School | Residuals for boys | |
	School (1998)	National (1997)
AT	–0.48	–0.46
AH	–0.44	–0.46
AA	–0.38	–0.46
B/A–E	–0.26	–0.46
B/A–R	–0.19	–0.46
BH	–0.01	–0.46
BL	+0.14	–0.46

It is clear that the schools in our A group are fairly close to the national residual for boys in French whereas the schools in our B group have residuals which suggest that boys are doing rather better than the national pattern for boys' performance in French. The table below shows how the schools selected matched the general criteria and the higher grade pass rate criterion:

| School Code | No. pupils | Age range | 5+ A*–C passes in French for | | |
			1998	1997	1996
AT	900	11–16	55	42	45
AH	1800	12–18	55	56	55
AA	1200	11–18	35*	50	52
B/A–E	700	11–18	62	55	65
B/A–R	1300	11–18	57	58	58
BH	1220	11–16	60	63	59
BL	1550	11–18	44	37	47
National average 5+ A*–C			46.3	45.1	44.5

* We knew that the dip in 1998 reflected a particular one-off recruitment strategy within the LEA; in 1999 the results, at 48, were closer to the pre-1998 running average.

A note on the dilemmas of matching schools to criteria

The task of matching schools to broad performance criteria in modern foreign languages is not easy; there are three observations we would like to make:

- The pattern of languages varies from school to school and sometimes from year to year. Although we aimed to focus on French, in one school that agreed to work with us we discovered that the main subjects alternated each year and in our target year the main subject was German rather than French. Nevertheless, for the sake of consistency, see figures above, we continued to present the school's performance data – which were the basis for its selection – for French.

- We looked for stability in patterns of higher grade passes over three years but there were some minor blips, sometimes a consequence of a change of internal MFL policy or, in one case, a one-off change of intake policy at local level.

- We discovered, during the field work, that one school was, for good reason (and seeking to dis-apply under Section 363) presenting MFL as an option in Years 10 and 11. In fact, because it was a popular subject at the school, 90% of the Year cohort chose to take a Modern Foreign Language but of the 10% who chose not to (about 20) most were boys. This will have made the residual in this school, where boys, contrary to the national pattern, were doing rather better in MFL, a slightly inflated figure.

Overall, despite the difficulties, we were satisfied that the schools identified by their LEAs as meeting our criteria included schools which reflected the national pattern (i.e. boys doing less well in MFL than in other subjects) and schools where boys were doing rather better in MFL.

2.2   The seven schools

The seven schools identified came from six LEAs across the midlands, south and east of England.

School AA is an 11–18 comprehensive school with 1,200 pupils, including 120 in the sixth form. A special feature of the school is its integration of pupils with hearing impairments and physical disabilities. The area it serves has a mixed catchment with service and light industry. The local business community is relatively affluent.

School AH is a 12–18 comprehensive upper school with 1,800 pupils. Located at the centre of a large and busy town, two thirds of pupils come from the immediate locality while the other third come from other parts of the town and its environs. About 20% of pupils come from non-European families.

School AT is an 11–16 comprehensive with 850 pupils drawn mainly from a white working-class area where there is high unemployment. Some pupils come from an inner city overspill estate. Few parents have pursued education beyond 16 and low expectations are the norm in the school's community.

School B/A–E is an 11–18 comprehensive. Pupils come mainly from the local agricultural community but there is also some light industry in the area. A number of parents have senior management positions and some have an international dimension to their work. However, there is some feeling in the local rural community that languages are not a priority.

School B/A–R is a large 11–18 comprehensive school. About half its pupils come from professional family backgrounds whilst about 30% of parents are employed in clerical positions and 20% pursue manual jobs.

School BH is a pre-1974 11–16 secondary modern in an urban setting with mixed industry. Over the years the school has changed its reputation and pattern of recruitment and its intake is now slightly skewed towards the more able; the school is currently over-subscribed.

School BL is a large 11–18 comprehensive on the outskirts of a dense urban area. It draws its 1,550 from inner city areas, some run-down estates but also from some of the wealthier suburbs. There is a substantial number of able pupils as well as a large number of pupils with special educational needs.

The project team is extremely grateful to headteachers and teachers for giving us access to data and for arranging times when we could talk with colleagues and students about the issues that the project set out to explore. We are also grateful to LEA advisers for helping to identify the schools.

2.3   Data collection in schools

A central feature of the project was the collection of the data from pupils themselves – mainly from boys but girls were also asked about their perceptions of boys' attitudes to and experiences of MFL as well as about their own experiences of learning in MFL. The two target years for data collection were Year 9 and Year 11 (i.e. just before GCSE work starts and the second year of the GCSE course). The project itself spanned two academic years. The Year 9 pupils who contributed were in the 1998–99 cohort and the Year 11 pupils (interviewed at the start of the new academic year) were in the 1999–2000 cohort. One field worker worked with three A and one B/A school and another field worker worked with one B/A and two B schools.

Data were collected in four ways:

- through discussion groups and individual interviews with pupils and teachers;
- through observation of MFL lessons in which the pupils interviewed were involved;
- through school and departmental documentation of policies, practices and results;
- through a simple questionnaire.

The **questionnaire,** which all Year 9 pupils across the seven schools filled in at the start of the research, was designed to give a rough picture of the extent to which boys and girls both enjoyed and valued the Modern Foreign Languages they were learning and to enable us to see whether there were differences between the sexes and between the schools. Pupils did not give their names, and to preserve confidentiality, forms were placed directly into envelopes after completion. The total number of successfully completed questionnaires was 1,266 (615 girls and 651 boys). Pupils indicated their enjoyment of and views about the importance of MFL on a scale ranging from **very enjoyable, mostly enjoyable, sometimes enjoyable** to **not enjoyable** and from **very important, important, fairly important** to **not important.**

Pupils' perceptions of languages as enjoyable

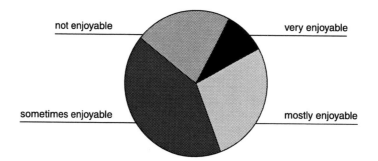

Pupils' perceptions of languages as important

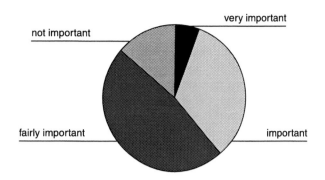

The findings showed that:

Enjoyable/Not enjoyable

French
Girls were significantly more likely than boys to find French **very enjoyable** and **mostly enjoyable.**

German
Girls and boys did not differ significantly in their opinions about the enjoyable nature of German.

Spanish
Girls and boys did not differ significantly in their opinions about the enjoyable nature of Spanish.

Important/Not important

French
Whereas girls were more likely than boys to feel that French was **important** or **very important** boys were more likely to feel that French was **not important.**

German
Whereas girls were more likely than boys to suggest that German is a **fairly important** language boys were more likely to indicate that German is **not important.**

Spanish
Girls were significantly more likely than boys to feel that Spanish is **important.**

The **lesson observations** were designed to enable the field worker to contextualise some of the data from the pupil discussions and interviews. The pupils involved in the **discussions and individual interviews** included:

- boys not doing well in MFL and thought to be switched off;
- boys not doing very well but thought to be engaged;
- boys doing quite well or well and thought to be engaged;
- girls who were average in performance and degree of engagement.

All the discussions and interviews were recorded and transcribed. The number of pupils who contributed across the seven schools:

	Y9 boys	Y9 girls	Y11 boys	Y11 girls
Discussion groups	42	21	30	12
Individual interviews	50	–	42	–

In each school, interviews were held with the headteacher or a deputy, the head of department and four MFL teachers (in all, seven Heads or their deputies, seven Heads of Department and 28 MFL teachers). At least one MFL lesson was observed in each of the schools

2.4   The focus and boundaries of the report

- A distinctive feature of the project was its concern with **perspectives on learning in MFL gathered directly from pupils**. Teachers' perspectives on boys' performance in MFL were also gathered along with information on departmental policy and planning issues.

- In some of the schools boys were performing better in MFL than the national average; others were performing at or near the national average. However, the pupil data did not show clear differences between the different groups of schools; rather, there was similarity of views across the boys involved as to what made learning difficult in MFL and what were the conditions for effective MFL teaching and learning.

- The different patterns of achievement may be accounted for to some extent by (i) the capacity of more teachers in some departments to meet the conditions for effective MFL learning that boys identified; and (ii) by a stronger departmental ethos, with more consistent practices across teachers (the second observation is speculative and would need to be examined more fully in subsequent studies).

- The resources available for the study did not allow the research team to collect and analyse data in terms of (i) the socio-economic background of pupils, their ethnicity, the effects of parents' or carers' attitudes to learning MFL, and (ii) how coaching, bilingualism and multi-lingualism affect motivation and performance.

- While some girls were interviewed in each of the participating schools – and offered interesting observations on boys' learning in MFL – the focus of the study was boys' experiences of MFL learning. We do not think that the key points emerging from the data would lead to action which would disenfranchise girls. However, teachers could need to check out the perspectives of both girls and boys in their own schools on the principle that 'using research means doing research'.

2.5   The organisation of the report

To achieve coherence, **the boys' perceptions** of their experience of learning MFL are grouped under three main headings which emerge from the data as significant:

- the distinctive nature of MFL (**Chapter 3**);
- classroom interactions and interpersonal relationships (**Chapter 4**);
- boys' awareness of what helps and what hinders their learning (**Chapter 5**).

The **teachers' perspectives** are described in **Chapter 6**.

Summary findings and recommendations are given in **Chapter 7**.

Appendices include:

- an expanded version of the summary findings for use in **INSET or departmental discussion (Appendix A)**;
- a questionnaire devised from the report and used to discover more about one school's Year 10 pupils and their attitudes to learning an MFL (**Appendix B**);
- what a review of the literature (to 1999) tells us (**Appendix C**).

3 The distinctive nature of Modern Foreign Languages

Introduction

Responses by pupils and teachers to MFL learning and to its place within the curriculum have frequently been variable and not without controversy. Of the interrelated factors which inform understanding and shape experience of languages in school, the relationship between MFL and other school subjects and the particular demands and tensions which impact on pupils and teachers in an MFL classroom are especially significant.

3.1 Particular characteristics of MFL

3.1.1 Organisational frameworks

There are three areas which characterise MFL in school. There is firstly the emphasis placed by the National Curriculum and GCSE on four discrete but interrelated skill areas of listening, reading, writing and speaking which are assessed separately mostly in the target language and which relate to a specific Programme of Study. Secondly, in the GCSE, there is the need for accuracy if communication is to be considered completely effective. Thirdly, learning an MFL can be seen as the cumulative acquisition of linguistic information, which cannot be negotiated.

Given this framework pupils have a two-fold objective:

they must strive to:

- learn the language structures (content);
- use these to interact with MFL speakers (communicative competence) and make them part of their behavioural repertoire (Gardner 1985).

The data highlight the complexity of the MFL classroom, as defined by pupils' perceptions and the challenges it poses. The data further suggest that the demands are compounded when a second foreign language (L3) is learnt in parallel with the first (L2). While individual participants forefront particular concerns, across cohorts a typology emerged to represent a general picture of pupils' perspectives which relate to their understanding of the special nature of MFL and the problems that it may present to them as learners in school.

3.1.2 Content

This has a different focus from other curricular areas:

> ... in other subjects they give you a topic ... tell you the facts and you learn them ... in languages you learn loads of vocab. or you learn lots of sentences and questions. HAS3:11

> ... French is just so different to every other subject that you do at school ... it's something that is not happening in England ... it's a different country ... the surroundings ... the way the society is. TE3:11

3.1.3   **Language is broken down into independent skills with specific demands.**

Listening

> ... is incredibly hard because they throw in words you haven't learnt or they speak too fast but I suppose it does help ... a tape you can play back ... but I find it easier to listen to a person talking to me 'cos you can always ask them to slow down. AJE:9

> ... Mr X says French is so fluent that's what makes it easy ... but because it's so fluent everything sounds the same. AB:9

Reading

> ... it's all about picking up key words and if you get a key word you're fine. AJE:9

> ... a lot of the words we haven't learnt and it's hard to distinguish which ones we know and which ones we don't ... we usually work with somebody ... both of us understand some words and we use the dictionary if we can't work it out ... sometimes you disagree and it is even more confusing. AFB/A2:9

Speaking

> ... it is the pronunciation that's really hard 'cos you've got to get the accent right before you can even start talking about it. AJE:9

> ... you have to go further than saying 'I played football' ... .you have to explain ... sometimes it can get a bit difficult ... it's 25% of the final grade. L:11

> ... you have to practise it as much as you can ... it would go straight over you otherwise. EJ:2:11

Writing

> ... it's probably the hardest because you have to get the spellings right. ET1:11

> ... it's complicated because of the accents. AR1:11

> ... I struggle with the grammar. EFBM2:11

> ... when you are actually writing it you're getting used to the language ... you can see what you're doing ... you can go through it as many times as you like. HP1:11

3.1.4   **Language skills are interrelated and complex.**

> ... when we're writing it you have to put all these accents on but when you're speaking it you have to look at the accents and whether you pronounce the letters at the end or the beginning and all the different words you have to remember like female and male and polite and friendly ... it's so difficult to remember all of that ... there is so much speaking reading and writing ... in the actual French book we learn from they make it sound so hard ... they put everything in so much detail and with people like me and a few other people in our class we can't put all that detail down. HRS:9

> ... I need to learn vocabulary ... I need to practise saying the words and how they work within a sentence ... moving verbs about. EM1:11

3.1.5   **Grammar content is rule-based.**

> ... I chose German because I thought it was easier ... but the sentences are all muddled up and it's quite hard to figure out which part goes at the end of the sentence. EFG/M:1:11

> ... rules have to be looked at more regular ... you tend to forget the rules. L:11

Languages have specific, non-transferable language rules which have to be made explicit in MFL learning. These must then be adopted by learners for effective communication to take place:

> ... I don't study the rules frequently enough ... I don't use them properly. RCC:11

> ... I get confused in French ... 'cos it gets a bit complicated. AT1:11

This process in their first language is unfamiliar to pupils as it is subconscious and spontaneous and most pupils have little grounding in English grammar:

> ... it's totally different from English ... you are learning something totally different. RSH4:11

3.1.6   Each language has a particular system and structure which is different from another.

> ... I tend to put it from English into French instead of looking at what I've actually learned. RCC4:11

> ... you have a sentence and then it's all backwards and the last word is at the beginning ... it's complicated. TT:9

3.1.7   A standard model of the MFL is generally presented in school.

> ... we learn textbook French by the rule and everything ... when we speak English we don't speak it properly ... everyone has their own dialect ... and it would be nice to learn how they really speak it. RLD*:11

3.1.8   All lexis is new.

> ... there are so many words to learn ... it is just remembering them. EFBC3:11

> ... you don't quite understand what you're doing as much as if you were in English and Science ... it's harder to learn a new language than to build on something that you already know. RTC5:9

3.1.9   Proficiency in MFL is cumulative, developmental and requires perseverance.

> ... in Years 7 and 8 it was vocab ... in Year 9 we started to learn structures and Years 10 and 11 putting the structures together. RCC:9

> ... you write it down and don't look at it but you forget it after a while ... if you do the practising it stays in your mind more. AR:11

> ... when you don't understand you have to look things up in the dictionary and it takes time. HCH:11

3.1.10   The provisionality of MFL language acquisition makes demands on long term memory.

> ... there's so much to take in ... in Science you build on things that you've done in Year 7 but with languages it's like you're learning new things all the time ... OK, you're using the same structures and sentences but you're learning different vocabulary and it's hard to adjust. REJ*3:11.

3.1.11   Proficiency requires continuous practice ...

> ... in French we've gotta speak about it all the time and we've gotta keep going back through it because there's so many words ... in History you can sort of remember a bit of what you've learnt and then the rest will come back but it don't work like that in French ... because the words are all separate ... you can use them in different themes ... but you've got to learn them all separate. HJJ:9

3.1.12   **... and higher level cognitive skills.**

... with other subjects you can just write what you want in English but with French you have to stop and think about it. HCH:9

3.1.13   **A considerable amount of information has to be acquired; progression is not fixed.**

Certain content appears to have greater resonance with pupils, and more relevance:

... I think you should be taught ... the basic things on how to get by in France or Germany ... 'cos it's all very well being able to say that I have a brown dog but it's not very good for ordering a meal ... to really get anything effectively you have to learn everything ... it's just a case of trying to figure out **what** should be taught first ... obviously there must be some things that are more useful than others AJE:9

3.1.14   **Sound literacy skills in L1 are necessary for good performance.**

... I find it hard to spell and read in English ... in German it's even worse. TT:9

... I am better at reading and writing things in German because these are the things that I am better at in English ... that sort of transfer across. AP1:11

3.1.15   **Rewards in the classroom are more likely to be for accuracy rather than for ideas ...**

... it is totally different from English ... I've got loads of good ideas but it's knowing how to link them. RSH4:11

3.1.16   **... and differences of sophistication between L1 and L2/3 may be frustrating.**

... I try to write too much ... too detailed which I haven't got the language for and it ends up getting poor marks. RCC4:11

3.1.17   **MFL learning makes particular demands on individuals to establish working practices upon which successful performance is dependent ...**

... in groups in Languages you tend to mess about more because you don't quite understand what you are doing as much as in English and Science ... it's harder to learn a new language rather than build up on something that you know. RLD*:11

3.1.18   **... and requires pupils to be organised and systematic, and able to refer back to notes and rules.**

... I've got a French folder ... I've got to write it all down ... I've got to look in a dictionary ... it's getting through all those pieces of paper that I've got in my folder ... and it gets a bit frustrating when you can't find the right piece. HCH:9

3.1.19   **Learners also have to take responsibility for learning outcomes and to work independently in MFL.**

... homework is harder than other subjects because none of my family can explain it to me ... so I am really left on my own ... it is really hard if I get stuck. EA2:9

... you've got to learn the language ... you've got to motivate yourself to do it. RLD*:11

3.1.20   **Teaching an MFL lends itself to particular teaching styles and different classroom relationships.**

... the teacher just stands at the front teaching you ... compared with Tech ... where you are allowed to wander around and they are more friendly. LRP3:11

... I don't like the teacher ... the way they teach and personality ... she just dictates it all in German ... in French she makes it more interesting ... we'll join in. TT:9

3.2 Communicative competence

The communicative aspect of MFL learning poses further personal and psychological challenges:

3.2.1 Pupils have to speak clearly and in public.

... I tend to get myself across better in other subjects ... when I am speaking I tend to mumble a bit. RCC4:11

... I don't like speaking French in public ... it feels weird ... it feels like everything in your mouth is wrong. AA1:11

3.2.2 There are emotional considerations which may impinge on a learner's confidence.

... I'm a self-conscious person at heart and I get that when I'm speaking languages ... obviously if you go to another country that what you **have** to do. AP2:11

... I'm not very confident when I speak ... even in English. RLG4:11

... I don't like speaking in class ... in case you get it wrong ... then everyone is going to laugh at you. AJG:9

... German is a very speaking subject ... if you are no good at confidence then you can fall down ... somebody can be very good at the subject but not a very brilliant communicator. TFCGE:9

3.2.3 Engendering a positive approach to communicating with native speakers of the MFL and developing empathy requires particular skills and commitment.

... if you are going to use the language you are going to have to go to France and people aren't going to start speaking very slowly to you to make allowances for the fact that you're English ... you've got to get used to it. EA2:11

3.2.4 Cultural awareness is important for effective communicative competence.

... if you are going to talk to them (the French) you need to know a bit about them so you don't say something completely wrong. ARS:9

... they should try to make the Germans sound a little bit more interesting and talk about their actual lifestyle ... what they do and what we don't ... some German history ... not just how to pronounce certain words on a tape recorder ... it's better to know about the Germans themselves ... Germany has got a good history ... because at the moment we're just learning about a language ... we know hardly anything about them. TT:9

3.2.5 Positive experience abroad may contribute to, or reinforce successful performance ...

... I just like France ... I like going there ... it gives you a sense of achievement when you can say something to someone in French. LFP7:9

... the people who haven't been to France find it harder than ones who have. EAS:9

3.2.6   ... and motivation ...

> ... I did visit Germany this summer ... it helped a lot ... I've been keeping in contact with my German partner so I will work more on my German. 3HN:9

3.2.7   ... but linguistic 'surprises' may occur in the foreign context.

> ... it's weird because they've got different accents and what you learn in class is not really any help when you get there ... they speak very quickly as well so it's hard to understand ... but you do pick up the occasional word which you've learnt. TT9

> ... when you actually go to France you find that they are quite colloquial and you won't understand what they are saying. EFBM4:11

The artificiality of the school context, which especially relates to interaction in MFL between inexperienced non-native speakers and within the UK, may create further tensions for some learners who have already experienced going abroad and using the MFL for real:

> ... speaking French in school ... you feel a bit weird ... you are doing it because you have to and not because you want to ... in France you do it more because you want to ... the things you **want** to say not what you are **told** to say ... that you need to use ... useful phrases ... in school you treat it as a joke and **there** it is more serious ... I remember more of it when I am in France. EJ1:11

This may, however, be successfully mediated by foreign language assistants (FLAs):

> ... I like speaking with a real French person (the assistant). LDK4:11

or to a teacher who is also a native speaker:

> ... I've got a German teacher who is German so that helps a lot ... rather than having things out of a textbook we learn it as Germans would say it ... so maybe it's a little more realistic. AP:1 11

> ... Mrs X tells us a lot about what France is like because she is French. HR8:9

Most pupils must operate within an unfamiliar cultural frame. They are also entirely dependent on the teacher for their knowledge of MFL and on the teacher's skill to impart their own enthusiasm for, and expertise in the MFL to the pupils. Teachers must do this whilst working within the prescribed methodological and structural requirements imposed by the National Curriculum and GCSE syllabi and using the target language as the main teaching medium. Such requirements may further distance pupils from relating MFL to its local context and to their needs.

Pupils have problems where the focus is on areas that appear less meaningful:

> ... some parts are really silly ... and you don't need to do them ... but it is just that the teachers reckon it is on the curriculum and they **have** to do it ... I don't really think that they do. EFGM5:11

Additional problems are created by tasks which would be inappropriate for speakers in L1:

> ... we were given a sheet and some of the questions were like ... what colour would your father like! HFGL 5:11

... or tasks which encourage use of L2 in circumstances that seem implausible:

> ... in French they teach us some stuff that isn't really relevant ... we talk about going to play round someone's house or something like that ... I'm not going to go to France and go round and play round someone's house and start having a conversation with them. EFGL5:11

> ... I don't think that it is really stuff that you **need** to know on a visit to Germany in the future ... you are not going to need to know how to say about the school day, are you ... I can't see where that comes in useful as stuff like asking directions and things which are obviously useful ... if you end up in Germany. AP3:11

... a lot of stuff we learn is useful ... like how to talk in bars ... ask for the menu ... ask directions ... which is what you would need wouldn't you if you go over to France ... but then some stuff I don't think is very useful like learning about housework and stuff ... like ask someone to do the hoovering ... I don't think that's useful to go to France. L:11

3.3 The second (or third) foreign language

3.3.1 Learning a second MFL (L3) can be a very different experience from the first MFL (L2).

... French ... seems a lot harder at first to German which is why most people choose German at Options ... but French does, I think, get easier ... whereas German starts off easy and then it gets harder and you go into all the '*der, die, das*' and so on. ALC:9

3.3.2 The complexity of learning one foreign language may be compounded, not facilitated by learning another one.

... learning two languages at the same time is very hard ... it's hard to cope with ... say if you're learning the months in French you will be learning the months in German and you get confused ... same with colours and numbers ... it's harder when you first start learning ... they interlock them ... every time you do say *time* in French there will be *time* in German ... it's just hard. ADC:9

3.3.3 L3 may interfere with L2.

... it gets confusing, especially if you are doing the same topic in each language (e.g. *cinema*). RLG3:11

... quite a lot of people who are in my group all answering questions and it's the right answer but it's in the wrong language. ADC:9

... it's like confusion within the two lessons ... one day you have German ... then French the next day and you've then still got German in your head ... it's hard then. HBH:9

3.3.4 L2 may be preferred to L3 or vice versa because of the nature of the tasks ...

... my German's more boring than French ... it's textbook work ... lots of *Gute Reise*. ... you have to read out of a book and write the answer ... it's just really boring exercise work ... it doesn't really stick in your head at all ... 'cos after a while you think ... let's just get it over with ... you don't actually take in the information. AJG:9

3.3.5 ... or the content.

... in Spanish we do how you're feeling ... how many brothers and sisters have you got ... in French it's normally boring stuff like *time* and that ... which isn't interesting ... French I find a bit dull. HCH:9

3.3.6 There is the further complexity of the perceived degree of difficulty or interest in one or other language ...

... after Year 8 I didn't get interested in French ... just lost interest ... German is good fun ... I like it ... In German I try and in French I don't work much ... I don't enjoy it and I find it much harder than in German ... German, I suppose, sounds more English. ALC:9

3.3.7   ... and differences in teacher style and relationships.

> ... I don't mind speaking German because I enjoy it ... my German teacher doesn't seem to be as strict as my French ... if you do some work wrong you don't want to be shouted at. HDG:9

> ... I don't like German ... it's hard to learn ... I don't like the teacher ... the way they teach and personality ... she just dictates it all ... in French she makes it more interesting ... we'll join in ... she makes us join in ... she makes you say stuff even if you don't want to. HNT:9

3.3.8   Motivation and application to L2 and L3 may differ.

The first foreign language may form part of the active language repertoire and social experience of individuals outside school whereas the second foreign language may not have the same status. Motivation and application to L2 and L3 in school may differ:

> ... the majority of my parents' friends know it (French) and ... it's like a natural thing ... but German ... it doesn't agree with me ... it's just a tough language. I never have to use it and I just learn it in school ... I've never had to apply it anywhere ... I see some point with all this Euro business but **now** it just doesn't seem any point of it. ADC:9

3.3.9   However, pupils exposed to a range of languages *outside school* may develop learning strategies that can be constructively implemented in learning L2/L3 school languages.

> ... I speak Gujerati and English and depending who comes round I can speak different languages ... Arabic ... Urdu ... Punjabi and a little bit of Hindi ... my Mum and Dad have a wide range of friends so I pick up stuff ... when I listen I pick out key things I need to learn ... then I adapt them and I figure out that means that ... that won't make sense if that's not that. HJS5:11

3.3.10   Negative attitudes towards the country where L2/L3 is spoken may also impact on performance.

> ... I don't work much in German because not many people do ... not to be horrible to German but ... all the Adolf Hitler business ... we're doing about Adolf Hitler in History at the moment ... not many people like German very much and they tend to muck about a bit. HFB:9

3.4   Other factors that are critical for MFL

Organisational factors such as class size, the potential for individual monitoring and attention, seating arrangements and working partnerships, as well as the gender balance and gendered working practices of the group are also critical, although they may not be exclusive to MFL.

3.4.1   Class size can be critical.

If classes are too big, pupils suggest they flounder because of linguistic and interactional constraints.

3.4.2   Seating arrangements.

If imposed by the teacher, these may impinge on pupils' working and coping strategies. Success in MFL may also be influenced by the selection of appropriate working partners for pair work/group work. Pupils need to feel comfortable with someone they know, otherwise pairwork or group work may be threatening.

4 Classroom interaction and interpersonal relationships

Introduction

Good relationships, mutual trust and respect are fundamental to successful learning in school. Conflicts of expectations and tensions in these relationships impact on the dynamics in class and on the learning that takes place. The interactive and communicative demands of MFL and associated tasks that are essential practice in the classroom make demands on pupil–pupil as well as teacher–pupil relationships.

Researchers have attempted to identify the learning strategies adopted by successful language learners (Rubin, 1975, Stern, 1975). O'Malley and Chamot (1990) categorised these strategies into three groups:

1 metacognitive strategies that involve planning and evaluative learning;

2 cognitive strategies that involve confronting the language itself;

3 social and affective strategies through which the learner interacts with others or controls his/her own emotional response to the learning situation.

To promote successful MFL learning in school and to provide opportunities for these strategies to be developed, teachers have to establish and develop a rapport with their classes and to create a positive, supportive environment in which learning can take place. The teacher has also to function as a model for the target language as well as encourage pupils to empathise with the target language community and its cultural context. In addition, teacher–pupil relationships are influenced by the rigours and pressures imposed by the National Curriculum for MFL and GCSE syllabi and examinations. The four discrete language skill areas – listening, reading, writing and speaking – must be accommodated with equal emphasis and with their own focus, each requiring different relationships with and between pupils, and different classroom dynamics. In listening, pupils adopt a receptive role, for example, whereas in speaking the teacher has to encourage the pupils, not just to speak, but to listen and react according to prescribed procedures and around topics dictated by the syllabus. Some pupils describe these arrangements as unnatural and unrealistic and are hesitant to perform. Learning an MFL in school does not always appear to relate to using the MFL in a real context.

The MFL teacher has to monitor, diagnose and target pupil progress individually and collectively to enable pupils to perform accurately and effectively. The emphasis is on language use.

> … in Science it's something that you already understand but you need to understand further … which you can just take out of a book … but French … you can't read a book about French and then all of a sudden speak it fluently … it depends on the teacher to get it stuck in your memory. RAB5: 9

Boys see a lack of real content in MFL: as an object of study it is 'all words not substance'. This contrasts with other curricular areas where teachers can allow pupils to reach their own understandings in an exploratory way by using English as a means of communication. The process, focus and language are different, so different relationships are encouraged and ensue.

Key issues relating to classroom relationships emerge from the data. They relate to both cohorts and have implications for both Year 9 and Year 11:

4.1   In MFL pupils recognise that they are particularly dependent on their teacher.

4.1.1   Effective teaching and learning rely on good management, clear lesson structure and careful organisation of tasks by the teacher.

Good management is based on good relations, themselves an interactive dynamic dependent on pupils' application and receptiveness, an appropriate attitude, and sharing responsibility for learning.

> ... a good teacher is not just a person who knows the language well but is able to relate that across to the whole class ... being able to appeal to the people who are good and those who are bad ... she makes it fun ... she's got personality and it really comes across when she's talking her language how much she loves teaching the subject ... which makes you more enthusiastic to learn ... to be able to speak to her ... and to know what she's talking about ... HSD*7:9

4.1.2   Teachers need to be competent, enthusiastic users of the target language ...

Pupils appreciate that they are particularly dependent on teachers' confidence and competence as linguists and communicators to provide an authentic model, and to supply accurate knowledge of structure and lexis as well as appropriate cultural background. Boys recognise that their confidence relates to their success.

4.1.3   ... and able to promote independent and successful learning.

Pupils are reliant on the teacher to create appropriate ways of working which in turn enable them to be more independent. Teachers who do allow learners to be more autonomous may enable pupils to become more confident as a result. Harris (1998) found that there was a general concern with boys about the lack of independence offered in MFL classrooms compared to maths or physics where they were required more often to work things out for themselves. This data also suggests that some boys were motivated by a sense of ownership of process and outcome, but usually in close association with the teacher whom they felt they could consult freely to mediate their concerns. Pupils' perceptions of their own success are particularly important in this area.

> ... it helps if you know you're good ... you have more confidence and you're not afraid to ask questions in class. HJB:9

4.2   Pupils have clear expectations of teachers based on their understanding and experiences in MFL classrooms.

4.2.1   An effective teacher has a good rapport with the class, listens to and understands individual pupils, and ensures learning takes place by creating positive working relationships based on mutual respect.

As highlighted in previous research (Clark and Trafford, 1995), teacher personality and successful classroom practice emerge clearly from the pupil interviews as significant, but, unlike Powell and Batters (1986) teacher gender does not. Pupils respond primarily to a teacher's personal, individual and relational qualities. They measure teacher skill by his or her ability to gain respect and establish successful working relationships in class. This is an interactive process which is unpredictable, yet dependent on several interrelated factors. Once a pattern is established it is likely to become fixed.

> ... it's a mixture of things ... it's obviously whether you get on with them or not ... on a base level ... and whether you think they are a good teacher ... if you don't think they are teaching you anything valuable or teaching you as well as they could then obviously you are going to lose respect for them ... and it is basically whether you **connect** with them ... if you see what I mean ... if you get on with them and you understand what they are saying and they understand what you're saying ... it is not a thing that you can plan for ... it is something that just happens ... within the first couple of lessons of having a teacher you have basically decided whether you like him or her ... or whether you don't ... it is not something that changes very much over time. AP5:11

4.2.2   Boys respect management that is consistent, firm and fair.

Boys suggest that they are more likely to be engaged by language tasks set by a teacher they respect. Performance is enhanced when this respect is mutual. However, the balance between establishing clear parameters and being too strict is critical and boys are more likely to take advantage of the teacher if such parameters are not made clear.

> ... we had a new teacher at the start of the year ... he didn't seem strict ... you could tell ... you can always get away with more things and they don't always notice. HN:9

4.2.3   Boys respond well to skilful managers with additional personal qualities that engage and motivate; being happy, well informed and able to create a relaxed atmosphere promotes learning as well as interesting content.

> ... having a certain type of teacher helps because last year I had some guy from Germany and it was the worst lesson you could possibly imagine ... it was very strict but you can't really do that with languages ... now I've got a different German teacher and it's sort of uplifted it a bit ... the atmosphere ... that's all it is ... and you've got to have a certain kind of teacher to generate that atmosphere ... sort of bright happy easy-going ... in silence that's the worst thing you could possibly do. AJE:9

When the teacher generates an atmosphere in which boys feel comfortable in class and at ease with the language, this also makes them want to take part.

> ... someone who obviously has a very good knowledge of what they are teaching ... someone who can put across what they are teaching in an informative but not overly structured manner ... not just pounding the information into you but giving it some variety and ... making you interested in it ... I think that is the best quality a teacher has to have ... they have to be able to get you interested in a subject ... 'cos if you are not interested in it ... you are not going to listen ... you're just going to muck around you're not going to pay them any attention at all ... so they **have** to be able to get you interested in it ... and therefore they have to be interesting themselves ... they have to be able to get you to pay attention ... so they have to create the interest. AP5:11

4.2.4   Predictability appears to be an important feature of classroom interaction.

Changes in pattern or routine can set off resentment or induce lack of respect:

> ... you associate certain activities within the classroom with the lesson ... it is very routine-based ... it's completely irrational but that's the way it is. E54:9

Sudden changes in seating arrangements, for example, were felt to have a marked impact on pupils' relations towards each other and the teacher. They felt less at ease. Teachers also reported that although pupils may listen more if they, the teachers, were in control of seating, there was no 'atmosphere' because pupils were less likely to interact with others. This is important in a subject with a significant communicative element.

4.3   **Relationships are variable and some boys may be particularly sensitive to the learning environment that obtains.**

Breakdown in effective communication can impact negatively on performance and pupils who feel insecure with their teacher are less positively engaged.

4.3.1   **Boys respond well in relationships that are consistent and stable, where all pupils are treated as equals.**

Boys are critical of arrangements where, in their view, particular pupils are patronised and treated differently because of gender, or marginalised because of their ability to understand and perform. Some boys interviewed felt that teachers interacted primarily with more able pupils in the class and were less likely to involve those who routinely supplied incorrect answers. Others felt, like those reported by Jackson and Lahadenne (1971) for example, that, if they misbehaved, they were more likely to receive harsher and more negative comments in general than those directed at girls guilty of the same offence.

4.3.2   **However, most boys claim that they engage differently with the learning environment in MFL than girls.**

> ... with boys when something is boring they just switch off but if something is interesting and they want to learn about it then they try and they put effort into it ... girls ... they just do it anyway ... they work because they think they have to ... they're not bothered if it is interesting or not ... they work because they think it is important. LFBH:9

Boys confirm that they are less likely than girls to adopt and maintain the sound study skills, good presentation and thorough learning strategies demanded of them in MFL. They are less inclined to concentrate, memorise, listen to others, follow instructions and work constructively with peers and are more reliant on the teacher to motivate them to communicate and interact in the target language.

4.4   **Boys' attitudes affect relations in class.**

> ... your approach to your work is pretty important ... you have to have a good attitude ... it's up to you really, isn't it ... if whoever is doing it decides ... oh, I can't be bothered ... they **won't** ... and if they go ... yes, I'll be bothered ... I **want** to do this ... they **will**. HAF:9

4.4.1   **Boys see their willingness to work as being dependent on good relations in class, on the teacher's attitude to them and on his or her teaching style.**

In the data it is clear that pupils often perceived a teacher's attitude to be reflected in their approach to management. Typically, boys equated authority and respect with caring teacher attitudes, but some pupils concluded that poor management also reflected indifference.

Attitudes such as these have implications for motivation and performance. Teachers who are lively and enthusiastic, transmit and transfer this to the class. Boys, in particular, respond well to humour, variety and fun. Pupils suggest that motivation and feelings of success are mediated through relations in class. Whereas Year 9 pupils said that they were particularly motivated by praise, albeit on an individual and private basis, Year 11 pupils sought the teacher's encouragement in a less specific way. The teacher's focus and concern about their progress, however, was a key factor in their motivation.

4.4.2   **Attitudes, however, change when working relationships break down.**

A breakdown in relationships is often triggered by boys who are disinclined to participate. In response, teachers may make pragmatic rather than principled decisions, leading them to employ strategies which enable them to cope but which may not foster good personal relations:

... teachers shout if you don't understand because everyone in our class is naughty. LFG:9

4.4.3   Some pupils resent the disruptive behaviour of boys.

Some pupils expressed their frustration at being in a disruptive class, showing empathy with the teacher, but still being drawn in by others who were not engaged:

> ... I find it funny but it is my education they are ruining ... 'cos they are really stressing her out ... I told her to calm down and not to bite every time they are being silly ... she has calmed down and generally she's much better. HFB:D8:11

Negative attitudes are also reinforced and develop over time, with serious consequences in Year 11:

> ... it was a new subject in Year 7 ... I suppose I was **good** at it when I was in Year 7 ... if you're good at something then you usually want to carry on doing it ... but if you're not particularly good at it and it doesn't interest you then ... what's the point ... why would you want to do well ... if you've got no chance ... I **hate** French ... I don't like it at all ... I would revise for all the subjects but French ... 'cos I don't even know if I'm going to even bother to come in for the French exam. HJ:5:11

The indifference shown by a small minority of boys in Year 11 to success in GCSE may also affect other pupils and relationships in class:

> ... I think that some people feel that they don't want to go into Further Education ... some of my friends ... they have got jobs set out that they are going to start ... so even if just a couple of people start mucking about that aren't really bothered about what grades they get ... it spreads around ... and then you just talk and you forget what you have been trying to plan to do in the lesson ... it is normally just a few people who aren't bothered ... and then everyone just joins in like sheep. TT5:11

For some this may become an excuse for poor performance; others may choose not to interact:

> ... I don't get detentions for clowning around or being rude or anything ... it's just being lazy really ... I'm in the top set as well. HFB/R:8:11

As within other subjects, pupil maturity is likely to be reflected in their attitude and relationships in class. Overall boys reported that they were less inclined to 'muck about' in Year 11 that they were in Year 9. There are clearly very different agendas at play with the impact of impending GCSE examinations being the main focus of the older boys' comments.

4.4.4   Some disillusioned boys recognise and can identify strategies to improve but see no need to succeed.

For some pupils, lack of success in their language lessons may not stem from them not knowing how to get better results; it may be that they see no reason for learning a foreign language or to keep working in their MFL lessons so do not bother to make the effort. They justify this attitude by blaming the teacher. It seems that some boys, in particular, are less inclined to take a proactive stance and take responsibility for their own learning:

> ... if I needed to learn French then I would have to sit on my own and try to concentrate a bit more ... this isn't the best class, it's all disruptive really ... the teacher is no good; she just don't care ... she lets us do whatever we want. TH1:11

4.4.5   Having specific, regularly assessed targets can affect the attitudes of learners, especially younger boys.

Year 9 pupils describe not only the positive effect of specific target-setting on their progress which otherwise may seem less purposeful, but stress the importance of their teachers' expectations that these would be achieved.

4.4.6   **An element of language choice for Subject Options can enhance the positive attitudes of some boys; this may foster better relationships within the group.**

> ... in Year 8 everyone did French ... whether they liked it or not ... in Year 9 you could choose whether you did German or Spanish ... so a lot of people who really didn't like it did it ... so they mucked around in the class ... but in Year 10 when you are taking your options the people who were doing French were people who had chosen to do that ... so that meant that more people wanted to do well in the French ... you didn't have a lot of people just mucking around in class who didn't really care what they had got ... so people worked harder in Year 10 and 11 because they wanted to do well. HFB/R:6:11

4.4.7   **Performance in class is affected by unpredictable factors which have consequences on pupil attitude; these may be both provisional and variable.**

Pupils mention time of day, day of the week, being tired and their mood as well as that of the teacher and others in the class as having an effect on their attitude and performance:

> ... I do work hard in lessons but obviously it depends on what mood I'm in ... sometimes I don't feel like doing languages and I won't understand ... if I'm in a different mood I'll be volunteering all the time to answer the questions. HNT:9

> ... sometimes you are tired and you can't concentrate and sometimes you're distracted. AJE:9

4.5   **Boys perceive that MFL lessons can lead to tensions in relationships.**

Pupils are aware of the language teacher's role which requires them to balance management of personal relations in the classroom with the methodological demands and assessment practices of MFL.

4.5.1   **Some boys were particularly anxious for teachers to maintain personal relationships within the group dynamic and pay particular attention to them as individuals.**

Unconfident and insecure in their ability to assimilate language structures, underperforming boys feel threatened by the MFL context and are particularly dependent on the teacher's skill at reducing this ambiguity through their explanations, tasks and enthusiasm for the language. In addition, they respond well if teachers approach them and interact with them directly as individuals, giving clear explanations tailored to their specific needs:

> ... when the teacher comes round to you individually she makes you think more ... that's the most learning that I do when she is coming round ... she spends a few minutes with me ... she'll talk to me and make me think ... then it will start coming back ... she don't give you the answer ... she'll make you think and you'll try to associate. HC2:11

For some pupils it is necessary for teachers to reinforce and mark that relationship by writing a personal language reminder on the board – a word or phrase, for example – which a pupil does not know. This helps them as an individual, rather than the class as a whole, and the attention is seen as encouraging, with the teacher taking a personal interest. If left alone such pupils were more likely to flounder, become distracted by social relations and engage in off-task or even disruptive behaviour. Such behaviour may, in turn, be another, equally effective strategy, from the pupil's point of view, in gaining the teacher's attention. It has been noted (Spender 1982) that boys receive two thirds of the teacher's attention in class but although much of this attention is negative and reflects discipline problems it has the effect of giving boys ' ... greater independence because they are interacting actively and directly with the teacher who is in turn taking their questions and behaviour more seriously than the girls'. (p91)

4.5.2   Boys respond positively to explanations when these are interactive, and to the challenge of a lively pace.

Some pupils showed concern that, when the main objective in a lesson was to explain a particular language point, teachers did not always adopt a dialogic or interactive approach. Pupils often perceive this approach as being insensitive to their pedagogic needs. In turn, it may compromise the learning that takes place. If, for example, a teacher always uses the same tone when giving grammatical explanations, all explanations begin to 'sound' the same and they seem repetitive. Pupils do not relate to these very much, lose concentration and 'drift off'. Then they no longer know what to do in class. When such explanations are routinely 'boring' a pattern is set; confusion is compounded over time. Such is the cumulative nature of MFL learning.

Boys also commented that if the pace is too slow, or if there is frequent repetition, language work seems too easy and not stimulating enough, so they lose interest and become disengaged.

4.5.3   Certain pedagogic practices in MFL can lead to disaffection, boredom and poor behaviour.

Some pupils did not recognise that particular topics in MFL were progressive and became more complex when developed at a later stage. Instead they were critical that these re-emerged, that they had already 'done' them, so did not want to pay attention. Such pupils often plateau and lose the willingness and motivation to progress:

> ... you don't become more sophisticated because half the time we'll just feel that it is so boring we won't pay attention ... so it isn't as if we could get to that higher level because we just sit back ... and yeah, we've done all this before ... what's the point. EFG/M:4:11

Pupils' lack of understanding and perseverance can also affect the dynamics in the class:

> ... they all argue ... it is usually ... I'm not doing this it's too hard ... and slam their pens down ... they don't ask for help ... they just slam their pens down and shout. TFG/E:6:11

Disruptive behaviour not only has an adverse affect on a teacher's pace it can also have a detrimental affect on the learning of the rest of the class:

> ... boys mess around in my class ... four got sent out today ... but it takes up a lot of lesson time ... half a lesson that took. LJW:6:11

Boys recognise that good teachers know the strengths and weaknesses of pupils and are able to command respect. Pupils then value their feedback which has a positive knock-on effect, boosting confidence and giving them control over their learning. Some pupils describe how, in other school subjects, this also enhances their performance.

4.6   Boys' relationships through talk

4.6.1   Speak but don't talk; an ambiguity particular to MFL.

Learning a modern language is talk-based. The language model is presented orally and part of the teacher's role is to encourage pupils to talk. Talk is also a means of establishing and maintaining relationships as well as practising language structures. Teachers and pupils sometimes have different understandings of the parameters of talk as a productive strategy. Pupils' assumptions about the appropriateness of talk can also be different from the teacher's; encouragement to speak has to be reconciled with a taboo on talking in class.

Which language to use – target language or mother tongue – is also crucial. Teachers must actively encourage on-task talk where pupils' response to the teacher is in the foreign language.

However, when pupils work with others their response is often in English. Research has shown that the ambiguity of a task can be reduced by 'scaffolding' a pupil's understanding (Bruner in Mercer: 1994) through talk. Like Vygotsky (1962), some pupils maintain that 'negotiation' (Mercer, 1994) in English not only refines their mutual understanding of concepts which become clearer as a result, but extends it, thus enhancing learning:

> ... one of the reasons that makes languages a little bit easier is your friends and you discussing the work ... 'I think this but what do **you** think?' ... and you eventually get the right answer between us ... but if there's deadly silence it's 'shall I put that in?' ... 'shall I not put that in?' ... if someone's doing it with you it's easier ... we don't copy exactly ... but we just discuss it between ourselves. AJE:9

For this process to be effective, it has to take place in English. Some teachers, however, may not recognise that this is beneficial or necessary in an MFL lesson. Talk as practice, and speaking as a response, are encouraged, but such 'around task', metalinguistic talk, may be confused with 'off-task' social chat, particularly if English has no approved place in that MFL classroom. Teachers may also be less inclined to allow the use of English in class in order to maintain more effective management and control.

4.6.2   Talking in MFL lessons for examination practice may be seen as an unnatural use of language in what may be an ambiguous social setting.

Because a foreign language is assessed in discrete skills the parameters of the speaking test in oral examinations are clearly defined, and what pupils perceive as conversation in English bears little resemblance, in their view, to a conversation in the MFL. Topics are primarily chosen by the teacher. Knowledge of a range of tenses has to be displayed by pupils, and responses are measured against specific criteria designed to assess linguistic competence and sophistication rather than the ideas pupils wish to express.

In Years 10 and 11, in particular, speaking practice has to be encouraged in class around the topics prescribed by the GCSE. Teachers, however, cannot monitor all of this all of the time, and speaking can indeed be a pretext for off-task talk. Boys are quick to realise this and some say they only perform in MFL when the teacher is nearby. Talk-based work may then provide the space for 'mucking about'.

4.6.3   For some boys their teacher's use of the target language as the medium of classroom interaction is seen as self evident, natural and beneficial for their learning. For others lack of comprehension can cause problems.

In accordance with the requirements of the National Curriculum, teachers are encouraged to talk in the target language. If relationships are good using the target language is not an issue; indeed it is perceived by pupils to be an additional benefit. It only becomes problematic when individual pupils do not understand:

> ... sometimes they babble on in French and I haven't got a clue what she's going on about but the rest of them have ... others get down with the work and I can't do it ... I have to ask. LRH3:11

This affects individual pupils differently. Some teachers may not, at times, adapt their teaching and their working practices to accommodate some pupils' needs. This may then have an adverse effect on relationships. Those teachers, however, who modify the language, adapt the speed with which they talk, or implement other strategies to share meaning develop positive relationships that give pupils a sense of achievement and success, and encourage a greater willingness to concentrate and to be involved.

4.6.4   Motivation, especially for younger pupils, can be enhanced by communicating with others abroad.

The reality of the target language is also contextually based. This resonates differently with different pupils. Relationships with speakers abroad through contact with 'real' foreigners were still seen as an important feature by Year 9 pupils. The likelihood of such contact in the short and long term also has a motivational effect. This appears to be less relevant to Year 11 pupils who were more concerned with requirements of the GCSE and less with the creative, communicative use of language outside the classroom and abroad.

4.6.5   **The success of pairwork and pupil-to-pupil talk seems to rely on friendly partnerships with a collaborative rather than competitive way of working.**

The impact of teachers' control on working arrangements and classroom organisation such as seating and grouping, also impinges on relationships that are established through and because of talk. Being assigned to work in a group is very different from naturally forming into one.

Although the asymmetry of teacher–pupil discourse is well established, it would be misleading to assume that pupil/pupil discourse is the equal partnership suggested by Fisher (1993). Pupils recognise that peer relationships are variable and the dynamics of friendship are particularly significant:

> ... I don't know many people in my French class ... there is only three other boys ... when the teacher says 'get in pairs' there is me left over because I don't really know any of them ... I usually get put with nobby-no-friends that no one want to go with. HFB/R:3:11

The success of many MFL activities is dependent on how comfortable pupils feel with their partners and relies on mutual trust and co-operation. Teachers may attempt to foster team work, co-operation and involvement but these are features of relationships often beyond their control.

The benefits of pairwork arrangements are described by boys. They felt that these were less likely to be threatening and intimidating, especially when working with someone of the same ability, and particularly with a friend. Performance is not judged so harshly, mistakes are acceptable and monitoring is mutual as they are 'on the same wavelength'. It is easier to make language decisions concerning appropriate lexis and the accuracy of structures because understandings are reached jointly and collaboratively. Individuals can be more specific in a one-to-one arrangement because they are not competing for voice. This, in turn, is less distracting.

Some pupils felt threatened by working with someone more proficient and less trusted. Working together also became more difficult when relations were not equal or when they became competitive. Overall, pupils seemed to prefer self-selected partners.

Pupils who found it difficult to keep up were embarrassed and even humiliated when their lack of competence became apparent and inaccuracies were jeered at, not reduced. Pairwork which serves as practice for performance can also prove problematic if one partner is disinclined to perform in front of the class.

4.6.6   **Group work and working in mixed gender groups are seen as less successful ways of working.**

Group work arrangements were less popular with boys as these were seen to provide more opportunity for pupils to lose concentration, become confused and engage in social talk. The dynamics are more variable and complex, relying on initial and eventual enthusiasm for the task as well as being dependent on the individuals in the group:

> ... someone has to take charge ... some don't want leadership and some don't want to work. RSL:8:9

Although some pupils saw benefits of collaboration in productive problem-solving, others felt that their input was not valued; communicating their opinions became a struggle for voice. Those who were disengaged saw this as a particular benefit, as there was less effort involved and less French to speak.

Contradictory ways of working also relate to gender. Some boys in Year 9 describe their frustration in mixed gender groups deriving from the different working practices of girls:

> ... girls always tell you what to do in groups or they do it all themselves ... they won't bother with you ... we can't take the credit ... we don't know what we've done. LFBH:9

Others draw different conclusions:

> ... I think girls prefer to be told what to do and don't really like thinking ... they just like writing it down and revising it. RLD*:9

4.7   The impact of gender on relationships in class

4.7.1   When girls outnumber boys:

Relationships within the class often depend on the gender balance of the group. When left to their own devices pupils report that they generally form gender polarised groups in the classroom. In some classes where there were more girls present, groups of girls were seen to dominate proceedings. They were described as loud and arrogant but also charismatic and were able to manipulate proceedings according to their concerns.

4.7.2   When boys outnumber girls:

Boys tended to dominate lower sets. They were often louder, more physical, more difficult to manage and more demanding; they also needed more attention and more individual help if they were to perform well. Boys and girls point out that the disruptive boys are more likely to be in such groups because they do not want to work. The larger the class the more problematic this is and the more dependent on the teacher's ability to cope. The data suggests that the breakdown of relationships is generally triggered by boys' demands, which subsequently shift the balance of control. As a result some teachers either implement coping strategies, for example, asking the class to copy – in so doing often compromising principled MFL practice but 'containing' such boys and reducing confrontation – or they capitulate and accept defeat. Whichever outcome, pupils' expectations of the teacher and MFL become fixed; relationships as a result become increasingly difficult to modify.

Peer relations are not only divided along gender lines but by groups of individuals with similar attitudes or friends. In some instances, disengaged learners put into sets inappropriate for their ability but designed to move them from their friends, felt completely lost in MFL and totally discouraged. Such pupils were more likely to blame the teacher for a breakdown in communication and were often not willing to accept responsibility for their own poor MFL performance which resulted. Although pupils ascribe more importance to their teachers' personalities than their gender, teachers' expectations of pupil interaction principally reflected gendered behaviour stereotypes.

4.7.3   Boys' and girls' behaviour, relationships and working practices differ; this may lead teachers to treat them differently.

Boys' conversations with boys are more physical and loud, often concerned with establishing personal reputations and maintaining superiority. Girls' relationships, on the other hand, are closer, more personal and co-operative, and principally more passive. Accordingly, some pupils felt that teachers treated the boys and girls in different ways:

> ... in most classes girls are treated better than boys ... they behave a little bit different in the way that they are not so loud – try a bit harder and work a bit. TB:24:9

Girls conclude that it is the way the boys behave that lets them down:

> ... the boys used to be a lot worse ... girls seem to mature earlier than boys ... they've learned to control themselves ... they've learned when to stop. RLD*:9

Boys also recognise that they may behave differently from girls in class, but were less likely to see this as problematic:

> ... the boys do normally put their hands up for things more often whereas the girls are more quiet because they don't join in as much. ARS:9

Some boys have social and academic objectives which are not compatible with successful MFL outcomes and may be underperforming as a result. They often have difficult attitudes, and, from their descriptions, were clearly overtly negative, even aggressive and obstreperous in class. From the data they appear only to cope with short-term objectives and are not interested in paying attention to detail, concentrating on explanations, learning or reinforcing work for homework. They were often unsure of what to do in class.

4.7.4	**Pupils hold the view that success in MFL is not dependent on gender; boys, however, may sometimes go about it in different ways from girls.**

Boys do not always conform to stereotypical patterns. Boys who perform well appear to be more passive and co-operative; their relationships and practices closely mirror those ascribed to girls. Contrary to the suggestion by some teachers that there is a natural antipathy towards MFL in boys, some boys are extremely enthusiastic, see a wider relevance and are eager to progress. In Year 11 they enjoy the interaction and take responsibility for their learning:

> ... we don't just sit there and be quiet while the teacher says stuff ... we answer the questions ... we're working harder. RLG9:11

Macoby and Jacklin (1975) maintain that boys are more susceptible to peer pressure than girls. Pupils interviewed for this investigation suggest that girls are equally likely to conform to peer demands and expectations, but, unlike some boys, these are more likely to orientate around success in academic goals. Boys who aspire towards an anti-intellectual image may use opportunities offered through legitimate class activities to seek approval by their peers. Pupils agree that 'class clowns' in Year 9 are usually the same people wanting attention, who use the MFL activity to get a particular image across and who create a particular identity to establish credibility with their peers. They like to be the centre of attention so people laugh at them. Indeed, some teachers suggest that these 'class clowns' are often more popular with the girls who collude with them.

Although this behaviour may become less prevalent as pupils mature and with the onset of GCSE, Year 11 pupils reported that such elements of performance were still apparent. By Year 11, however, reputations have become firmly established and boys were concerned to maintain the status quo. Disengagement, it seems, is essentially public and mirrors negative attitudes and inappropriate performance in MFL.

4.7.5	**Public performance, such as role plays or pupil directed activity in front of the class, is not only a practice strategy – it also impacts on the atmosphere in class.**

Many boys prefer to be physically active, and are often perceived to be more imaginative and spontaneous than girls. Boys who perform well use this to their advantage. Channelling their energies into constructive MFL activity also deters some boys, it seems, from engaging in off-task behaviour; it may also motivate them to succeed. Boys in Year 9 were, seemingly, more willing to volunteer for such activities than girls.

Not all boys, however, are comfortable when performing to the class, some preferring to engage with others in a more private way in which they feel they have control. These boys described their distaste at speaking the foreign language in public; they were less confident, and felt intimidated, nervous, self-conscious and shy. They were also particularly anxious about meaning and pronunciation, and felt vulnerable if they made mistakes in public, feeling that they might be laughed at by their peers. They were also concerned that the teacher might prolong their embarrassment by identifying individual weaknesses in the foreign language. These boys explained that it can be humiliating if teachers correct them and make them repeat correct French several times to get it right.

Being told what to say was at times seen as unnatural. Also inadequate performance was sometimes justified by boys when there was an element of compulsion or lack of autonomy and control over the content of such interaction:

> ... In France you say things that you want to say not what they tell you to say. EJ:1:11

4.8 Which boys underperform, what are the relationships that obtain and how does underperformance develop?

Identifying individual underperformers can sometimes be problematic. Although it is recognised that, in the classroom, teachers are more likely to respond to boys' behaviour than to their gender (Powell and Batters 1986, Mifsud 1993) teachers' informal assessment can still be based on fixed expectations and gender generalisations about boys which are strongly rooted. Even though at times teachers realise that some boys' inappropriate behaviour may stem from frustration caused by incomprehension of the foreign language or of the task, or may relate to recent events outside the class, or to a pupil's mood they may still equate negative behaviour, poor social skills, inappropriate interpersonal skills and an immature approach with disenchantment and poor performance. Teachers generally react strongly to poor behaviour even though, as pupils suggest, they may not recognise or understand the cause. If this occurs, tensions between teachers' assumptions and pupils' perceptions are compounded in a relational dynamic.

4.8.1 Boys of all abilities may underperform in MFL.

Boys who underperform are not necessarily only those who are openly hostile to MFL or to others in a class, or who are in a low ability group. Teachers express concern about a middle range of boys who are more passive and easily ignored. The performance of such boys has been investigated by Lee, Buckland and Shaw (1998) who suggest that their 'invisibility' does not necessarily imply a lack of educational purpose (p59). However, some boys maintain a low profile in class and avoid direct interaction with the teacher. They are quietly disengaged and are more likely to become bored. They suggest that they employ passive work avoidance tactics and coping strategies which are not recognised by the teacher. Such pupils imply that they are initially overwhelmed by the challenges posed in the MFL classroom, which they say are eventually not worth pursuing. This impinges on their performance and, as it deteriorates, the pupils become indifferent. Boys who do not dominate class proceedings and who are not identified by teachers as overtly talkative, difficult or usually off-task, describe how their performance is compromised as they lose track of the MFL in class. The opportunist, who does not want to get caught or to be seen as a trouble maker, but who, unknown to the teacher is not engaged by MFL, takes advantage of events:

> ... if the teacher's just droning on and on you think ... please can there be a break in this ... and then people start talking again and there is actually a level of noise ... and you think ahh ... this is my chance to talk and not get caught ... sometimes you get the chance to chuck a ruler at someone you don't like ... and they come back and chuck it back at you ... and it hits you so you hit them ... I suppose it's just boredom ... and then the teacher suddenly goes ... and you think ... **what** ... what has happened ... (you) ask (someone) in front of you ... what does that mean ..and you think 'help somebody' ... tell me ... it destroys the lesson probably ... you can ask the teacher and then they tell you off for not listening. AA:3:11

Some boys describe how they may be overwhelmed by the MFL and just get quietly lost:

> ... some of the work is difficult ... if you don't keep up and then you go on to the next piece of work and you are already two bits behind ... you kind of get lost in lessons. HNT:9

> ... if it's hard I end up copying my neighbour's 'cos I don't know what to do myself. HFB/R:3:11

Others felt very strongly that because they were not overtly demanding they were marginalised and ignored.

4.8.2   Boys' poor performance as a downward spiral

Boys respond to a productive atmosphere, good quality teaching and management but in a difficult learning environment, they may employ coping strategies detrimental to good performance. Girls, however, appear to put up with a problematic learning environment and quality of teaching in a more passive way.

Boys who see no relevance in MFL, and who are not motivated through their relationships in class, lose track of the teacher's purpose and the language progression involved. This may lead to a deterioration in performance which is difficult to correct. The active use of the target language by teachers may also be a contributory factor when pupils do not make the moves to try to understand. Although for motivated pupils, as has been said, it reinforces lexis and structures and encourages their productive use of the foreign language, for others, the target language may reinforce incomprehension and lead pupils to go off-task. As soon as disengagement in MFL lessons becomes an established pattern, and when pupils are indifferent to progress, a downward spiral in performance becomes inevitable.

Michèle Deane (1992:44) illustrates how a teachers' unrealistic objectives can impact on motivation in MFL. Underachievement spirals down through low self-expectation and feelings of 'what's the point?'. This leads to low co-operation and low motivation which creates discipline problems in the class.

However, it is not only unrealistic objectives that trigger disillusion, but a range of complex factors caused by particular events. These differ for each pupil and may change relationships within a class, albeit temporarily. What is particular to MFL is that understanding and progress is cumulative, so pupils who become off-task quickly get lost and without considerable individual help given by the teacher, who is the only model for the language they have, it is difficult for them to get back on track:

> ... if you don't understand the work you can't get on ... if you don't get help ... you can't try – therefore you do nothing ... you mess around. LRH3:11

5 Boys' awareness of what helps and what hinders their learning

Introduction

Boys identified teaching and learning strategies, classroom activities, lesson content and a learning environment which, in their opinion, help them as MFL learners. As with all other aspects of this study these must be seen in the context of the schools in which they are learners, and as a sample which is not necessarily representative.

Although, overall, pupils are aware of gender issues in school and describe gender polarised working practices, gender is not seen by them as relevant to performance. This is more likely, in pupils' views, to be dependent on individual aptitudes, attitudes and motivation.

Pupils are particularly insightful in their understanding of their pedagogic needs. They are clearly able to identify their own strengths and weaknesses in MFL as well as related learning strategies and working practices. They also outline what, in their view, helps or impedes their learning and are able to describe effective or deficient teaching strategies.

5.1 Effective teaching strategies

It appears that some learners consider as successful, teaching strategies which set up efficient ways of working and thus allow them to learn, practise and consolidate language in all skill areas. For other learners successful teaching strategies are those which enable them to cope with what may be problematic classroom situations such as maintaining relationships with peers. For some pupils this may be more significant than learning the foreign language.

Most pupils are critical of teaching where language learning procedures are not made explicit and when these are not enforced because of weak classroom management. Learners are also critical if they find themselves in a situation with which they cannot cope; this is seen as the teacher's responsibility whether the pupils choose to be compliant or not.

Boys perceive effective teaching strategies as being dependent on certain classroom conditions:

> ... maybe if the teacher changed the way the lesson is done ... like don't let people mess around and make them do the work, and keep them working ... if people around me weren't like messing about and distracting me ... then I could do some more work. 19ANE:9

and on the teacher to generate an appropriate atmosphere:

> ... I think having a certain type of teacher helps ... the atmosphere, that's all it is ... and you've got to have a certain type of teacher to generate that atmosphere ... sort of bright happy easy-going I think.
>
> ... Interviewer: ... so not total silence?
>
> ... JE: No, that's the worst thing you could possibly do. 3AJE:9

An ideal teacher is one who makes the purpose of the work explicit and who is precise when explaining and setting the task: a comment on a teacher setting homework substantiates this point:

> ... she gives it to us to help us understand ... she explains it really well and it is always related to what we have been doing in class that day. TFGH4:9

It also helps if the teacher is in a good mood when starting and conducting lessons!

5.2   Effective learning strategies

Learning is seen as dependent on teaching style and what the teacher decides the class should do:

> ... it's the way the teacher teaches, you basically get ruled by what the teacher does, how he does it or she does it ... your lesson depends on what they want you to learn. 19ADC:9

Effective practice is unsurprisingly determined by individual needs seen in the context of and as being dependent on successful learning and teaching:

> ... it always helps if your teacher says 'oh, you're doing well', more than just yourself thinking it. 8ADC:9

What is apparent from a number of the interviews is the ability of the learners to perceive quite precisely what their particular needs are and to relate these to their personal strengths and weaknesses. Boys know that successful learning is dependent on them being in a working mood and on their determination, as well as on the ability of the teacher to create an atmosphere which facilitates their learning. Significantly, however, their mood and their determination are provisional and dependent on personal circumstances and interpersonal relationships.

Boys' observations identify and make explicit successful language learning strategies which they see they can put into practice collaboratively or which may be developed on their own.

Collaborative working, mostly casual and not formally organised, is mentioned in terms of the positive outcomes derived from getting help from others and working with a competent friend. Working together is also appreciated in specific skill areas: in writing, for example, boys see discussion with other pupils as making the activity easier. Asking a friend is also less effort for some than asking the teacher:

> ... I can't be bothered to ask the teacher so I just ask the person next to me ... they are pretty good at French. HFB/R:3:11

For other pupils working on one's own has its advantages. Some boys have developed successful individual learning strategies: memorising words and text is helped by saying the language a few times:

> ... you can only learn it when you speak it ... like it gets into your head. 9AJD:9

Others decide that to write down what they hear is a useful strategy.

In reading, some boys have developed an awareness that:

> ... it's all about picking up key words ... quite entertaining really. 9AJE:9

Personal weaknesses are clearly identified. In writing, the correct use of accents can cause problems. In speaking (French and German), pronunciation is difficult because learners feel that they have got to get the right accent; in their view this is helped by pairwork and making little plays.

When listening to the foreign language, boys realise that they have to listen several times:

> ... I know it's useful ... I probably benefit from it without actually knowing it but it can get tedious ... it's an important part ... it's repetitive ... I know it's really, really boring but it's useful, I think, and like that kind of makes you think, oh, well never mind, better get on with it. 11AJE:9.

Not all boys, however, adopt this pragmatic approach. Although they know what they should be doing, quite precisely at times, and what they have to do in less language-specific terms, underperforming boys acknowledge that they are often not working hard enough. Other learners are more specific:

> ... the way I approach my learning could be better ... I could stop mucking about and listen more and concentrate more when I'm doing writing work. 19AJD:9

It is significant that even pupils identified by their teachers as underperforming are able to recognise and describe strategies which would help them improve. However, despite this level of awareness many pupils thus identified are unprepared to help themselves and take responsibility for their learning and its improvement.

5.3   Classroom activities

There are a number of reasons why some activities are preferred by boys. Criteria relate to:

Difficulty

Some activities are preferred if they are perceived as easy:

> ... role play ... it's the easiest. AC1:11

Activities are also considered unproblematic if the content is familiar. Easy tasks, however, do not always appeal. If difficult activities are seen as a challenge some boys respond positively, for example when speaking the foreign language to the teacher:

> ... that's the only time you ever really have to think. When you're doing the sheets there's nothing to it. HC:9.

Enjoyment

Some activities are preferred if they are perceived as fun and if the teacher uses a sense of humour when working with and responding to the pupils.

These forms of positive motivation which underperforming boys mention and use to explain what supports effective learning are more likely to operate if activities are based on success, or based on fun:

> ... I've always wanted to speak another language ... I'm not that good at it ... it's just fun, I guess. TFBC2:2:11

Games combine these two elements: a game such as lotto is effective:

> ... because it's easy ... if it's complicated it loses me. AS2:9

> ... lotto ... easy and fun ... it's like you already know it. AA2:11

There are additional factors:

Self image

An activity can be preferred because other activities, in comparison, are more likely to make pupils look uncertain or embarrassed in front of their peers. Speaking can be embarrassing so writing may be better than speaking because it is less threatening than, for example:

> ... speaking out ... attending ... I don't like to make mistakes ... I don't like speaking out in front of the class ... everyone listens and then you don't feel so confident ... if you said it to the teacher ... one to one ... put in two's you'd probably be a bit more confident and you'd do it better. TT2:9

Relevance

Some activities may be preferred if they are seen as usable in a real life situation in the foreign country, or, particularly for Year 11, if they help explicitly with the GCSE examination.

Pupil control

An activity is preferred if learners feel they have control over the pace or if it can be performed independently of the teacher and if they, the learners, are active; moving around the room, making posters, putting up displays are mentioned positively.

Some few pupils have no preferences:

> ... I don't dislike any ... there are some that I prefer to others ... some that are really hard ... I can get some but (some) are a bit confusing. AS2:9

5.4   Pupil motivation

It is clear that, for the majority of boys, preferences can be prompted by particular types of motivation. Gardner and Lambert (1972) define motivation to learn a foreign language as being **instrumental** 'if the purposes of language study reflect a more utilitarian value of linguistic achievement' and integrative, 'if the student wishes to learn more about the other cultural community because he is interested in it in a open minded way' (p3).

The data illustrate several aspects of **instrumental motivation**: reading aloud can help pronunciation; listening and responding to teachers' questions helps recall:

> ... you have to think back ... it refreshes your memory. AR1:11

Oral work and speaking may be preferred because, in some pupils' opinion:

> ... talking would come in more useful. TT1:9

or it may help future job prospects:

> ... it's more interesting ... it is more important for jobs e.g. holiday rep. TM3:11

Listening carefully, although demanding, may be attempted more willingly by some Year 11 pupils to help ensure success in the examination:

> ... it helps me with my listening paper. HFG/G1:11

Integrative motivation is commonly mentioned in general terms:

> ... if I went to France I could talk to someone and be able to do normal things. JT1:11

> ... it is what you would use in France. AR1:11

> ... (on a visit to Germany) once you get the confidence up it's a lot easier to communicate with people. 1TRL:9

> ... I've been keeping in contact with my German partner. 3HN:9

or in terms of the value of developing particular skills:

> ... pronunciation is bound to help because you can go to a foreign country. TFB/C1:2:9

There is sometimes a realistic understanding that the way the foreign language is learnt in school is not going to be the same in the foreign country. If, therefore, integrative motivation is strong enough then the learners may make the extra effort:

> ... I find it quite hard but I like it ... if you are going to use the language you are going to have to go to France and people aren't going to start speaking very slowly to you to make allowances for the fact that you're English ... you have got to get used to it. EA2:11

In addition to the instrumental and integrative there are **other forms of motivation**. Some activities are perceived as helping classroom management and preventing pupils from misbehaving, and are preferred for this reason. The data frequently shows that boys like teachers to be firm and in charge. Controlled and well monitored oral question and answer activity, for example, means the teacher is orchestrating the activity and:

> ... you can't really muck about when you've got to speak all the time and you listen a bit more ... I think you get more out of it than just writing in your book because if you are not listening when she is trying to teach you how to talk and then she asks you a question you look a fool in front of the class ... so you want to know it and it interests you a little bit more. TT2:11

Similarly a **good working atmosphere** is essential, and this, too, depends on the teacher. This is seen as particularly important for listening:

> ... (a good lesson is when) everyone listens and works hard and everyone's quiet ... it's not hard to listen and pick things out. TT2:11

It is important also for speaking when the speaking is based on an oral model:

> ... because you can hear the things that are said ... it makes it easier to say it yourself. ET1:11

When discussing the four language skills further kinds of motivation are apparent. Some boys, although they experience problems, may nonetheless find that **an aspect of language learning is appealing**. In listening, for example, it may be the sound of the language:

> ... I like it but I can't understand it ... the sound ... it's alright. AS1:11

Or it may be the **challenge**: listening may appeal for this reason:

> ... (listening) is interesting ... it is a bit harder than some of the other stuff so it is a bit more challenging. HA2:9

Writing, too, can be unproblematic if it takes certain forms like copying off the board, or word searches, although as Heafford (1990) states activities such as these may be of limited value in language learning terms.

Boys are clear about what they like doing and are able to make their reasons explicit. Writing has a value for some because it is concrete and can be revised:

> ... you are actually writing it ... getting used to the language ... you can see what you're doing ... you can go through it as many times as you like. HP1:11 ... (writing) is more helpful. AS2:11

Display work is thought to be a helpful writing activity:

> ... it helps us to learn more because you have to look back through your notes ... so it is revision as well. TFG/H3:11

Posters have a learning benefit, too, because time is spent on **drafting and redrafting**:

> ... we do it over a week ... it is doing it over and over again so it stays in my head. TFG/D3:11

Sometimes the motivation relates to the learners' **ability to work on their own** and not to be dependent on the content or pace determined by the teacher, hence the appeal, for some, of coursework and worksheets:

> ... coursework – you can do your own thing and write it. HFG/F2:11

Worksheets:

> ... I find it (worksheets) easier in French (not in other subjects) ... rather than listening to the teacher. TFB/C1:2:11

Coursework does, however, rely on perseverance and research skills which may be less appealing to some boys:

> ... you've got to find loads of information and put it into French ... it takes quite a while to do. HFG/A2:11

Even textbook tasks, although not generally seen as easy, are acceptable because of the independence they offer. This may be enhanced if the learner is able to take measures not to be distracted by others:

> ... it's difficult (but) ... I prefer working from textbooks ... most of the work is individual and I actually like working on my own ... I find it easier in French ... I concentrate better ... I sit on my own as well ... out of choice. HT1:9

In this example there is a realisation that foreign language learning demands concentration which may be put at risk by other pupils in the class.

5.4   Factors influencing poor performance

Opinions about modern foreign language learning and its lack of appeal and resulting poor performance are multifaceted. These may relate to boys' perceptions of:

5.4.1   Difficulty

Boys say they do not like learning an MFL because it is hard. Perceived difficulty can come from a realisation that language learning takes times and demands concentration and perseverance, aspects which are significantly affected by classroom relationships and an individual's motivation to learn. This may be compounded if there is, in their opinion, a lack of interesting content:

> ... it's boring ... French! I don't find it hard ... I find it boring. EFG/M2:11 EFGL3:11

Difficulty may not always be general; at times pupils identify specific aspects which cause them problems:

> ... I'm not good at it ... I struggle with the grammar. EFBM2:11

5.4.2   Unclear purposes, unclear tasks

When learners do not understand why they are doing what they are asked to do they lose interest. They mention worksheets where they don't know what to write; copying:

> ... she writes a load of stuff on the board and you just copy it down then you don't really get to learn it, you just have it in your book to revise from, copying words we haven't seen before and (don't know) what they mean; copying from the board or OHP ... then doing gap fills ... it's boring. JT1:11

Unclear purposes may also relate to more wider considerations. Boys who, for example, are motivated to go to France may see little purpose in developing writing skills which they say they are unlikely to use.

5.4.3   Unclear explanations, unhelpful teaching strategies

The teacher's use of the target language is not perceived as creating problems when the learners are performing well. In fact it is rarely mentioned as an issue. Some boys even see the use of English as detrimental to their learning:

> ... they (the teachers) speak in English most of the time ... it would probably be more helpful if they spoke in French because we would get annoyed and then try and learn more. TT2:11

However, if the target language, rather than English, is used to explain a difficulty pupils perceive this as unhelpful:

> ... I'm copying stuff and I don't know what it means ... I ask the teacher and she explains in French and that doesn't help because you can't understand what she is saying a lot of the time. HFBR3:11

Explanations are, however, needed; simply providing an answer is unhelpful:

> ... when the teacher does help you she just tells you the answer ... she doesn't really teach us. HD2:11

Pupils need to think; they recognise that this helps their learning. More specifically able pupils mention that successful performance in MFL depends on their understanding of grammar; they comment positively on the value of grammatical explanation.

5.4.4   The nature of language learning

Boys sometimes feel that MFL lessons are pressurised and intense, especially if working in silence is imposed, a difference identified between MFL learning and other subjects:

> ... I don't think I could cope with silence ... it probably would be better in the end but it makes it a bit harder ... you feel too much pressure all the time ... it's like you're doing a test non-stop because you are in silence. TT2:11

5.4.5   The four language skills

Many boys are able to analyse the demands made by each of the four different language skills and can see where their individual problems lie.

Speaking

Speaking in front of the class, as has been mentioned, makes some boys feel self-conscious and less able to cope. This may, however, be seen as a challenge:

> ... it makes you work harder if the teacher says that you have got to do it in front of the class because you don't want to go up there and embarrass yourself. HFBR5:11

> ... some find it difficult to hold a conversation, but recognise that being able to do so is important. AP2:11.

Although the justification for an activity, such as language repetition, may be understood the activity may nonetheless be difficult to sustain:

> ... all this repetition stuff ... it goes over and over again ... I suppose it is to drum it in but it's boring ... it drums it in for that lesson but after a while you think what the hell was that. AA4:11

Listening

In listening they may know what to do but other problems may prevent successful strategies being used:

> ... (I know I'm) listening out for key words ... but they speak too quickly. EFB/M2:11

The speed of the speech in tape recordings is very frequently mentioned as presenting problems and creating a feeling of failure. Few pupils know whether the related tasks are designed for gist comprehension or for listening for detail. Were such objectives to be made more explicit learners may perhaps consider listening to be less problematic:

> ... it's too fast. EM2:11

> ... I don't mind it but it's difficult ... I don't pick up everything they say ... it's not what they say but the speed they say it. HP1:11

> ... the tape is always so fast and you never get anything ... everyone else seems to and you don't. ET2:11

> ... they say it quickly ... you can make out enough to know what they are on about ... but you couldn't really understand the whole conversation. TM3:11

Boys know that repeated listening does help comprehension but often find this tedious so are less willing to make the effort:

> ... you have to keep listening over and over again because they talk too fast and it is difficult for us to understand ... and that's boring. TFGE4:11

The only other problem in listening – and this is only rarely mentioned – is that of a regional accent which the pupils cannot understand.

Boys see listening as an activity in MFL lessons as different from listening in other subject areas. Listening to a teacher's explanations may bring its own problems of pupil concentration and interest:

> ... listening to the teacher go on about all the different things ... after a while it gets boring and you lose concentration and drift off and do other things ... it doesn't seem different every time she explains it ... it seems like the same thing and you don't really relate to it very well. AFBD2:2

But listening in an MFL has also to do with enabling the pupils to learn and then use a language model. If this is done effectively there is no problem:

> ... when you are listening the teacher makes you work harder so everyone gets on with their work. AJE:9

> ... listening to people speaking ... you can learn different things from when they speak. 9EB:9

However, if some pupils are slow to learn the model, for those who are quick the teacher's repetition may become tedious.

> ... say we are on a subject ... we have to repeat it too many times ... 'cos there might be some people in the class who don't quite get it, so you have to wait. HA1:9

> ... he just goes over stuff over and over again ... he does the same thing ... it is a bit boring. HFGA2:11

Writing

In writing, the problem-solving dimension may have an appeal but attention to detail is problematic:

> ... I don't mind working it out but I don't like writing it down ... you have to put all them funny letters in ... I find that hard and miss out all the accents. TBFC2:9

Some forms of writing can also be meaningless:

> ... I don't know what I'm writing about ... I'm copying stuff and I don't know what it means ... half the stuff I've written I just don't know what it means ... you steal phrases from the book. EM1:11

Copying straight from the textbook may not have a clear purpose and may be unrelated to more important skills:

> ... I copy without having to actually read it and then it doesn't help your pronunciation ... I prefer to know how the pronounce them. EM1:11

However, when the function of copying is made clear and when it serves as a means of improving performance copying was viewed positively:

> ... copying from a textbook is a good way of getting notes ... then reading them over (aloud) afterwards and any problems we have we can situate and then ask ... this will help us pronounce the words because that is important ... and also the meaning of the words. EM2:11

Reading

Reading aloud is seen to have little value. If it is used to promote correct pronunciation it does not, in pupils' opinion, fulfil this function effectively because:

> ... the texts contain a lot of the words we haven't learnt and it's hard to read and distinguish which ones we know and which ones we don't. AFBA2:9

Similarly, reading a text and answering questions has little interest, although some pupils perceive it as useful.

5.4.6   Other classroom activities

Several classroom activities, especially textbook exercises, are frequently seen as without a clear purpose and, as a result, appear in the pupils' words, unhelpful, boring, tedious, trivial or confusing. The purpose of exercises is often not understood; exercises with tenses appear complicated:

> ... 'cos they are using language which you may not have studied in classroom ... it can be a bit hard and it doesn't always work. EFB/M2:11

Significantly, for this study, boys appear to be less prepared than girls to complete tasks which lack interest and which they do not see as useful.

6 Teachers' reflections on boys and Modern Foreign Languages

Introduction

In each of the seven participating schools, four MFL teachers were interviewed for about 30 minutes each. The teachers included heads of department, newly qualified as well as experienced teachers and men and women. The first priority was to talk with teachers who were teaching the pupils involved in the study. A senior member of staff in each school was also interviewed (the head or curriculum deputy) in order to understand policy and progress in MFL within the overall context of school planning. However, in this section, the discussion is based on the data from interviews with classroom teachers.

Although the participating schools were variously successful in learning outcomes for boys, the views of teachers were broadly similar across the schools. There is no clear evidence of any significant or consistent differences in attitudes and opinions which might explain differences in performance in particular schools. Nevertheless, as we shall suggest in the concluding chapter, it is possible to detect in some of the schools a greater emphasis on work at departmental level and on aspects of classroom management.

6.1 Awareness of the problem of boys' underachievement in MFL

Among the teachers interviewed there was a widespread assumption that girls are likely to do better than boys and an acceptance that gender makes a difference, but no school had embarked on a clearly articulated set of measures to address the imbalance. Some teachers talked about the immaturity of boys relative to girls as a partial explanation of the difference:

> ... the girls seem to be a lot more mature, more focused on what they want in their futures and are quite appreciative that we are teaching them to the exam ... but the boys can't see beyond tomorrow, the boys don't realise the seriousness of it. B/A–E

> ... having told you that I try to treat them like adults, how immature a lot of them are, I must admit ... boys really ... very, very silly, they have always brought something with them that I have to take off them. AH

However, these comments did not reflect an unreadiness among teachers to give attention to strategies that are within their control. As one said:

> ... if that means we have to work harder to coerce the boys ... . then we will. BL

Teachers were clearly able to identify aspects of their usual teaching style that might appeal more or less to boys and girls. There was also a strong insistence on the expectation of high standards among all pupils:

> ... the teachers who take KS4 classes have very high expectations of all pupils, boys and girls, and are very good at frustrating the best efforts of the boys to be lackadaisical, badly organised and not do homework. BL

6.2 Teachers' understanding of the learning needs of boys

A clear consensus emerged from the interviews about what teachers need to give thought to if the needs of boys are to be met in MFL classes.

6.2.1 Variety of activity

The most common response focused on the need for variety of activity in the classroom. Teachers identified a range of things that could be used to ring the changes within the span of a lesson:

- Whole class directed work by the teacher;
- Role play;
- Group work (not so often);
- Focused reading activities;
- Listening to recordings as a whole class;
- Listening to cassettes individually;
- Using worksheets;
- Watching videos;
- Using ICT;
- Writing.

The balance of activities would vary with the age and ability levels of the pupils. The list above represents a range of possibilities and teachers warned against frenzied hyperactivity in the classroom which they believed pupils can find just as unsettling as extended concentration on one particular activity.

Teachers also pointed out that an activity such as writing, which, it is generally agreed, boys respond negatively to, can in itself vary in purpose and style. For example, it can be the written preparation of what will become a spoken dialogue; it can be a piece of creative yet semi-directed writing; it can be merely copying of vocabulary and it can be part of a comprehension activity. Some writing tasks may be more acceptable to boys than others. Both teachers and pupils recognised that writing can also be used as a class control mechanism rather than a genuine language learning activity.

6.2.2 Pace

Many teachers mentioned the need to keep up an energetic pace in the lessons. Teaching MFL is not a relaxing experience; concern about losing control and about keeping disengagement at bay requires MFL teachers to work themselves and the pupils hard by focusing on variety and pace. Several teachers mentioned the sheer physical demands of being a good MFL teacher throughout a full teaching day.

In terms of gender, teachers thought that girls were more willing to work at a steady pace whereas boys needed to be hustled into action and then the teacher had to work at sustaining a high level activity in case they switched off and engaged in counter-productive activities. As one teacher said:

> ... once they've done their activity and practised it a couple of times, they will start talking in English about other things which are not appropriate to the lesson. B/A–E.

It was clear that teachers felt the need constantly to be on their toes in order to ensure that such opportunities for distraction did not occur.

6.2.3 Physical activity

Teachers also talked about the need for physical activity within the lesson, particularly for younger boys. Restlessness can be channelled into creative activity or it can become a source of indiscipline. Teachers talked about giving boys the chance to move round the classroom in order to carry out interviews, to come forward to demonstrate a role play, to take part in a game which might involve standing up and sitting down, to engage in miming activities or to come forward to write on the board or use the overhead projector. Some teachers thought that an additional motivation for boys was to be in a position where they could command the attention of the class:

> ... they just love any opportunity to show off, basically. AT.

6.2.4   Competition

Teachers had clearly thought about harnessing boys' more pronounced fondness for competitive activities within language lessons:

> ... boys definitely respond better to active, exciting things, competitions and competitive games. AT

Teachers use games, challenges, 'beat the clock' activities and instant tests involving pupils competing with each other or a pupil competing with his or her own previous best. Some teachers talked about using competitive challenges of a grammatical nature in order to motivate pupils to get to the next level of language competence. In one school the teachers' concerted effort within a competitive approach was reflected in the pupils' accounts of what helped them to make progress.

6.2.5   Sense of fun

The teachers recognised that all pupils – but the boys in particular – liked it when there was an element of fun in the lesson:

> ... my policy is that if they don't enjoy it, they won't do it well. BL

It is difficult for teachers to set out to be funny and indeed there are control risks in doing so but some teachers recognise that they develop better relationships with pupils when they are able to have a 'bit of a laugh'. They also commented on the ways boys like to appear to subvert the lessons by introducing, sometimes, deliberately silly examples into classroom activities. What was less clear was girls' reactions to teachers who tolerate boys dominating the lessons in this way. There is a narrow dividing line between seeing such behaviour as a threat and as an opportunity. Some of the teachers were quite relaxed about allowing the boys to be funny because it can help build a spirit of comradeship within the group. One teacher said:

> ... you have to catch them in Year 7 where it becomes the norm to have fun in a language lesson. B/A–R

6.2.6   Explaining the grammar

More able boys usually want to know how the language works and are not easily satisfied by learning set-piece phrases, especially in relation to topics which they are not interested in:

> ... grammar, I think, clicks more. I'm talking about the top sets obviously. The boys are more logical and if you explain the structures and use lines and diagrams, the boys will respond more to that than the girls. BL

There is a dilemma for MFL teachers: how much to use the target language and teach 'communicatively' and how much to explain the grammar in English. Teachers appear to feel under pressure not to use English in the MFL classroom and many admitted to doing so with a degree of apology:

> ... we are not a department that tries to do everything in the target language because that's what someone has said is a good way to do it. We try to do whatever we think is most effective. In KS4 teachers delineate between when the target language is used within a task and when grammar explanations are given in English. They don't alienate the pupils by throwing a barrage of target language at them, which puts them off. BL

Whatever the source of pressure to maintain communication in the target language, it is clear, especially for those pupils who easily get lost but also for pupils who want explanations of grammatical structures, that teachers should feel comfortable in using the English language where they consider it appropriate in terms of the needs of their pupils or the nature of the task:

> ... I think it's a good thing to have target language but not the obsessive sort of approach that we were asked to adopt in earlier years. AA

6.2.7   A clear understanding of the purpose of the activity

Many teachers remarked on the perceived need of boys to have the purpose of classroom activities explained quite clearly. Whereas girls seemed to be prepared to work out what was expected (e.g. in tackling a worksheet or in pursuing a textbook-based activity) boys would frequently ask for clarification or reassurance that what they were doing was what the teacher expected. They seemed to need clear boundaries which would guide their efforts:

> ... they suddenly realised I was actually helping them because I had made it easy and accessible and they could follow. AH

6.3   Target setting

Teachers were ready to use target setting as a means of focusing attention and increasing motivation even, sometimes, at the expense of higher level aspirations:

> ... as a linguist, I love pupils to come in and be there for the linguistic experience but we are realists as well and we are target driven and results driven. So I often find that pupils being able to monitor their own (progress) does lead to raised levels of enjoyment and success. B/A–R

> ... if I actually set targets for boys in my form – 'you must achieve so and so by the end of three weeks' – they actually listen to that, they actually respond well to that. AT

6.4   Teachers' awareness of the pupils' dependence on the teacher in MFL and of the importance of interpersonal relationships

While it is clear that the ability of any teacher in any subject to establish a good relationship with individuals and the whole class is important, the teachers interviewed thought that this is particularly crucial in MFL where much of the work depends on the interpersonal activity of communication. Whereas in other subjects there is an external corpus of knowledge which teachers are helping pupils to understand, in MFL it is the interaction between teachers and pupils which is the medium of learning. This perception was also reflected in what the pupils said.

The irony is, however, that the essence of teaching a foreign language – communication – can become a barrier to the development of a good working relationships, particularly when the teaching is conducted in the target language:

> ... you've got to be careful because you've got to establish a decent relationship with the class and if you use the target language all the time you just can't do that. B/A–R

This dependence was also apparent in relation to the setting and completion of tasks. As one teacher vividly said:

> ... as long as I stand there with them and say 'do this, do that', they are able to do it, but as soon as I have to pay attention to someone else and I am not controlling them directly, they will do something else. AA

Boys need close teacher guidance and they need both stimulus and approval. Some teachers give approval in public by handing out merit awards, stars or even chocolate bars! Others prefer to give praise privately and feel that this is more effective, especially when pupils reach a certain age and do not want to be singled out by the teacher in front of their peers for fear of being seen as a 'swot':

> ... some of them desperately want to be praised but you can't praise them in front of anybody else because that's 'sad'. And that's not specific to languages. AA

Teachers expressed a predictable anxiety about teaching lower ability groups which were dominated by boys who enjoyed 'mucking about'. General lack of classroom discipline among the students was mentioned more frequently by cohort A teachers as a barrier to effective learning:

> ... I suppose mucking about is a form of reaction against a subject in which they have lost interest and enthusiasm ... which comes first, the mucking about or the loss of interest? AT

On the other hand, it was also noted that a teacher who can strike up and sustain a good relationship with a group of difficult boys can get a very positive response. The assumption therefore that low ability boys are always difficult to teach is not borne out by our data but it is also clear that achieving a good working relationship is dependant on the qualities and character of the teacher. The qualities that can be successful in such situations can also vary: sometimes strictness can work provided that pupils can see, behind the strictness, a human dimension – someone who is interested in them as pupils. Indeed, all pupils can sense whether or not a teacher has got to know them as individuals and whether he or she is responsive. Many of the teachers in our sample mentioned the importance of being available at the end of lessons and outside lessons to deal with the learning problems of individual pupils. This readiness to give up time was reflected in the pupils' appreciative comments about teachers who take trouble to help them.

Two quite different profiles emerge from the interviews of teachers whom pupils positively respond to. The first is that of the 'strict teacher' and the second is that of the 'ready to have a laugh' teacher:

> ... he is perceived as quite a scary person ... very directive, keeps a very tight rein on what is going on. They really do respond. The number who have opted for German next year from his group is phenomenal. BH

> ... I'm used to performing and cracking jokes ... it really worked with ... Year 11 group with some really difficult characters. I didn't go in cracking the whip. We established a relationship early in which it was clear to them that I was keen on their progress but I was also interested in them as people. B/A–R

Teachers often mentioned the importance of having a structured behaviour management policy that was operating across the whole department. They stressed how important it was for teachers to be seen to be applying the same rules, insist that homework is being done, carry out the detention regime fairly and consistently and expect tenacity and rigour in the work of both teachers and pupils:

> ... I think we've worked hard as a department to standardise our approaches, our pedagogy, our implementation of procedures and our ways of preparing pupils for the GCSE exam in particular. BL

In this project we did not set out to look at differences in learning attributable to gender differences among teachers although it was suggested in one school, where the pupils were seen as pretty tough, that women teachers tended to find them more difficult to handle than male teachers. It may be that the 'have a laugh' style and the 'strict but human' style are more readily within the repertoire of men teachers than women teachers.

6.5

Teachers' awareness of the link between motivation and success for boys

The teachers we spoke to were conscious of the need to motivate pupils to learn. This is true of all subjects but it is particularly the case in MFL where the subject is perceived by pupils to be 'hard'.

Many teachers mention the importance of parents in encouraging their children to work hard at languages. Parents who take pupils abroad, or who are able and prepared to pay for them to take part in study visits or exchanges, are seen by teachers as supportive. Reference was also made in the interviews to parents who come to parental consultation evenings. Not all parents are willing or able to do this and some teachers felt that they were fighting a losing battle for motivation where parents were indifferent or took a negative attitude towards language learning:

> ... I had a parent who came in to say they couldn't see any point because languages don't matter anyway ... and his opinion is reflected in his children ... we haven't got a leg to stand on. B/A–E

Teachers tended to think that girls accepted MFL as a subject on the same basis and with the same status as other subjects whereas the commitment of boys seemed to be more dependent on their perception of its relevance and utility. For instance, boys react positively to meeting a native speaker of a language:

> ... the simple fact of having somebody who speaks that language normally is such an indication to the kids that this is not something we've made up, that they have to do because we feel like torturing them, this is something genuine that happens in the world and therefore gives it validity. B/A–E

Teachers also pointed out that the fact that language learning is seen as something you can stop at sixteen appears to diminish its value in the eyes of the boys. If languages were really important, teachers argued, they would have the same status as numeracy and literacy, subjects that are perceived as having a very high status.

Aware of earlier research that suggested that MFL was seen as a girls' subject, some teachers spoke of the efforts they made to include male role models and to introduce topics which would capture the interests of boys. The topic areas for GCSE do not always serve teachers well in this respect since many of them are related to domestic topics, family life, school and interpersonal relationships. Teachers have to make positive efforts to direct the boys towards those aspects of the work which are to do with leisure activities or which may point to future job opportunities:

> ... they often ask, especially lower down, why are we doing this ... we are never going to go abroad so there is no point ... and I think that the units that we do – at the café, buying clothes and so on – are not masculine enough for them and that somehow turns them off. B/A–E

> ... boys always have to see the point. AH

Although there was some positive reference to the value of ICT for motivating boys, several teachers voiced reservations and sounded warnings about it not being the panacea that some teachers across the schools expect it to be. (We did not gather sufficient data across schools to allow us to elaborate on this issue.)

Seating was another issue raised by teachers and it was clear that they were aware of potential problems: for instance, if pupils are allowed to sit where they want, boys who are not motivated in MFL tend to drift to the back or edges of the room. Teachers feel that they need to intervene to change such 'natural' groupings – a move that pupils might resent – in order to ensure that pupils can work with a range of different pupils and in this way prevent anti-work cliques developing:

> ... I'm very keen on engineering the classroom. I move them on, I break up the friendship groups, I identify the key boys, the potential disruptives and the quiet ones. There was initial resentment but now they know what will happen when they come into my classroom. B/A–R

For reasons which were not entirely clear, the teachers interviewed were somewhat reluctant to make too much use of group work although they recognised that boys and girls can bring different and valuable qualities to such activity:

> ... the girls bring lots of qualities – like being very careful, knowing their stuff, not skipping – and the boys on the whole will tend to take risks and they will jump, they will often be more intuitive than girls. B/A–R

It may be that the tendency for boys to go quickly off task deterred teachers from making greater use of group work; what was missing perhaps was a sense that group members might develop responsibility for the work of their own group but MFL teachers tend to see themselves as the pivot of the learning and group work, where their authority is more diffused, may therefore not be so attractive.

6.6 Teachers' perception of the inherent and distinctive difficulty for many boys in learning MFL

The package of explanations that teachers offered for boys' less reliable progress in MFL can seem daunting: reference was made to boys social immaturity, their intolerance of what they perceive to be irrelevant subject matter or clear justification for studying a subject and also the intrinsic difficulty of making tangible progress. Not surprisingly, teachers were concerned about the greater opportunity, as they saw it, for behaviour problems to be initiated in MFL lessons by boys who were unable to sustain attention or who were avoiding situations where they thought they might fail. As one teacher explained:

> ... often with the lower groups it is a behaviour problem and it is not restricted to modern languages, but I think it is escalated in modern languages because we're encouraged to use so much speaking and target language and they find that difficult and that's when their concentration goes. AT

Teachers recognise that language learning is just not easy:

> ... I think we are very demanding in languages because we demand to look at detail and if they don't, they're lost, however much you dress it up with the song-and-dance act. ... . I think in other lessons, I'm not criticising other subjects, there isn't the constant demand. I mean, if they're not looking at me all the time, or listening to me, I'm not pleased and there's never any working for a length of time with a partner, or something they can get on with (on their own). It's always little tasks and they always need help. BL

There was some feeling too that the very nature of MFL, which tends to be managed as communicative, affective and relationship-centred, is inherently more attractive to girls than to boys:

> ... what has gone against the boys is that it is all about expressing your feelings, they don't want to touch that with a barge-pole, it really makes the boys cringe. BH

As one teacher said, boys seem to have a 'more natural antipathy' to MFL – and the challenge is to find ways of overcoming it.

7 Summary of key findings and recommendations for practice and policy

1 Boys see MFL as different from other curriculum subjects and as making distinct demands. Differences relate in particular to:

a the central position of the teacher in language classrooms (as model for language and culture, enthusiast, manager, and teacher);

b classroom interaction being predominantly dependent on understanding and using another language;

c the volume of learning in MFL that is based on language, rather than content;

d the emphasis on accuracy in MFL learning and the relative absence of opportunities to explore 'ideas';

e the complex and cumulative nature of MFL competencies, of having to persevere and the consequent difficulties of 'catching up' for those who fall behind;

f the importance of particular working practices on which successful performance depends

g the elusive nature of MFL as a subject and the lack of 'reality'/'relevance' that it has for some boys;

h the four discrete skills of listening, speaking, reading and writing.

2 Given the centrality of the teacher in the MFL classroom, the teacher's capacity for making and maintaining good working relationships as well as his or her pedagogic expertise is an important factor in boys' response to the subject and their willingness to work. Having a teacher whom boys would judge to be 'good' is an important dimension of engagement, especially in a subject where classroom work tends to be strongly teacher-centred.

3 Boys respect and want teachers who can make learning in MFL exciting and engaging and who can also maintain an orderly and purposeful classroom.   'A good MFL teacher', in boys' eyes, is one who respects individuals, who can engage pupils over the span of the lesson and across lessons, vary pace, find ways of involving them actively in their learning, find opportunities for some degree of choice, sustain an orderly and purposeful atmosphere, and have fun. 'Having a laugh' is not inconsistent with orderliness; what boys dislike are lessons where 'a bit of fun' escalates and the teacher is unable to get the class back on track.

4 Neither boys nor girls see MFL as strongly gendered (earlier research showed a stronger link between the subject and its gendered image).

5   Boys seem less concerned about whether a teacher is male or female than about the quality of the teacher.

6   'A good MFL lesson' is one in which there is a clear and explicit reason for all the activities which a teacher organises; this will include answers to why choral repetition, why pair work, why listening tasks, why writing and how these activities help learners learn and make progress in the MFL.

7   Boys recognise their own underperformance and can suggest reasons for it. Some believe that their individual performance can be improved if, for example, they have more ownership of content, task and strategy. A few see trying to improve as futile. For some, the potential for underperformance may have its seeds early on in their MFL learning in school.

8   Because the pedagogy of MFL is so teacher-centred, boys who are underperforming tend to see the teacher as responsible for the difficulties that they have in their learning.

9   Where boys fall behind in an MFL and feel lost or disoriented, 'messing about' is a way of responding; given the distinctive nature of MFL, the subject appears to be particularly vulnerable to such a situation.

10   Because of the cumulative nature of learning in MFL, underachievement, once established, is difficult to correct. Boys become caught in a downward spiral and can feel excluded; strategies for helping them to catch up and keep up seem to be particularly important for MFL classrooms.

11   Learning an MFL is, for some boys, an 'unreal' experience; the reality factor increases when pupils meet and can communicate with native speakers within school or on visits to other countries or cultural centres.

12   Learning an MFL is seen as 'hard' by many boys. The task of learning a second MFL in school is not necessarily experienced as easier since the second language's structure and conventions are usually perceived as different.

Recommendations for practice and policy

The recommendations relate to points (shown in bold) made in the 'Key Findings'; numbers refer to what boys said and the letter T to teachers' comments. They are formulated partly as a response to problems which boys identified in the study but had no answers for, and partly to reflect some of the boys' positive suggestions and experiences.

1 • Content for MFL

Create opportunities for learners to speak to native speakers – student teachers, a Foreign Language Assistant (FLA), other adults, other children – either face-to-face or via e-mail, FAX, or from a website. This may illustrate the 'reality factor' for learners, especially boys.

1a 1g 3 6 11

This may also decrease the centrality of the teacher in the learning process, provide engaging content some of which can be chosen by the learner, emphasise content as well as language, show the relevance of MFL when communicating fact and information, and link language skills more coherently.

1a 1c 1d 1g 1h 11

Encourage an exploration of the target language as both the medium and the object of study. The National Literacy project may have launched aspects which younger learners and their teachers can build on immediately.

1b 1d 1g

Create opportunities for an element of pupil choice in what is done in class and at home. This may help give pupils a greater sense of responsibility for what they do.

1a 3 8

2 • Talking to the learners

Talk more to boys and girls of all ages about what makes or could make learning an MFL a positive, worthwhile and enjoyable experience. This might offer insights into how pupils define activities which are 'engaging', 'purposeful' and 'fun'.

3 6

Trial and evaluate ideas designed to involve pupils more actively in their learning not only in the choice of content but also how to go about their learning – classwork activities (successfully completing listening tasks, adopting appropriate reading strategies, improving the quality of their writing, speaking), homework, memorising, independent study, etc.

1a 1c 1e 1f 1g 1h 2 3 6 7

3 • Explaining teacher intentions

Teachers can make more explicit from the first year of language study why they are asking learners to do what they include in lesson time and for homework – and what the teacher sees as the purpose of each activity (choral repetition, pairwork, writing tasks, listening to cassettes …) in terms of developing and improving language performance. This may help involve learners more in the teaching and learning process, demystify aspects of MFL lessons and explain the precise purpose of what pupils are asked to do.

3 6 7

4 • Repeating language models, explanations and instructions

If a teacher provides a language model for pupils to follow and use later, it is helpful if this is repeated to the whole class and to individuals at several different moments in a lesson. Giving instructions and explanations a number of times may help those when a lack of concentration or bewilderment prevented these being understood when first presented. Boys also suggested that if instructions and explanations were made interactive they thought they understood them better.

9 10

5 • Preventing a downward spiral

Provide strategies for pupils to catch up or keep up by trialling directed or independent study in school, precise and limited targets, self help using supplementary material, work with a FLA, extra individual guidance from an MFL teacher, departmental MFL 'surgery' times. Some of these strategies may not only prevent a downward spiral but help make learners more responsible for their improvement.

1e 7 9 10

6 • The relationship between learning a first and a second foreign language

Since boys see learning a second foreign language is not necessarily made easier by their experience of learning a first foreign language teachers could make more explicit links between the two. This may help explore and recognise similarities, where they exist, as well as illustrate significant differences. It was useful at times to compare mother tongue and the target languages.

13

7 • Departmental policy

Improved standards for all and progress by boys can be enhanced:

- By a clearly defined departmental approach aimed at consistency of practice (target setting, homework, rewards and sanctions);

- By achieving a high status and visible profile for languages within the school and by establishing live links with the local community and with foreign speakers.

T

8 Conclusion

'Boys' under-achievement – why all the fuss?'

This is the question asked by Delamont in a recent review (2000, p424). She argues, from evidence in a book by Epstein et al (2000), that 'the failures of boys have (long) been bemoaned' and that we are in fact dealing with a problem that has been around for some time. Helen Demetriou, in her longer literature review for the present study, refers to the 1693 treatise in which Locke argued that compared with boys, girls learned French rapidly and successfully using the conversational method that he had advocated (see Cohen, 2000). And, she adds, the Taunton Commissioners (1860s) noted that girls, attached more importance to the subject (French) than boys, were more anxious to learn and less disposed to ridicule the accent or other peculiarities of a foreigner' (in Bayley and Rouish, 1992). Delamont suggests that the current panic and hysteria surrounding boys' performance may have been generated as part of the over-arching concern about school effectiveness and failing schools.

So, the broad outline of boy's behaviour and performance patterns may not be new but there is, nevertheless, an issue to be addressed. Girls seem to have made faster progress over the last few years than boys (see Arnot et al, 1998) – and it is not unreasonable to try to find out why that might be. Our trust is that curiosity is driven by educational concerns rather than just the pragmatic concern to lift the school's performance profile because of the league tables. As one very successful Year 11 student said in an earlier study:

> … I don't think the school is interested in my grades because of me and my future but because of the school's reputation.

Members of the project team share the view that schools should not focus on boys' performance and attitudes to learning at the expense of girls. We are also aware that referring to boys' and girls' as two discrete groups is convenient but misleading: there are individual and groups of boys and girls whose experiences and performance are different from those of most of their male or female peers. We are also aware that teachers' professionalism is founded on a commitment to helping every pupil realise his or her full potential and in an increasingly global society it is important to ensure that all pupils have opportunities to do well in languages learning. Male and female pupils tend to acquire broadly different ways of interacting in class, different preferences and different patterns of work (see Warrington and Younger, 2000, p404). We need to understand these differences in order to ensure that teaching styles do not advantage some pupils or groups of pupils more than others. It is in this spirit that we carried out the study and drafted the report.

Bibliography

Andersson, B. E. (1995) *Why am I in school?*, paper presented at the European Conference on Educational Research, University of Bath, 14–17 September.

Arnot M., Gray, J., James, M. and Rudduck, J. (1998) *Recent research on gender and educational performance, a report for OFSTED*. HMSO.

Bayley, S. N. and Rouish, D. Y. (1992) 'Gender, Modern Languages and the curriculum in Victorian England'. *History of Education* **21**, 363–382.

Clark, A. and Trafford, J. (1995). Boys into Modern Languages. An investigation of the discrepancy in attitudes and performance between boys and girls in Modern Languages. *Gender and Education,* **7**, 315–25.

Cohen, (2000). In Epstein D. et al (eds) (1999*) Failing boys? Issues in gender and achievement.* Open University Press.

Deane, M. (1992) 'Teaching Modern Languages to pupils with special educational needs? With pleasure!' *Language Learning Journal,* **6**, 43–7.

Delamont, S. (2000) 'Three inequalities in search of a solution?'. *British Educational Research Journal,* **26**, 3, 423–4.

Erickson, F. and Schultz, J. (1992) 'Students' experience of the curriculum'. In: Jackson P. (ed) *Handbook of research on curriculum.* New York: Macmillan, 465–485.

Fisher, E. (1993) 'Distinctive features of pupil–pupil classroom talk and their relationship to learning: how discursive exploration might be encouraged'. *Language, Literacy and Learning in Educational Practice.* Multilingual Matters Ltd in Association with the Open University.

Fullan, M. (1991) *The new meaning of educational change.* New York: Teachers' College Press.

Gardner R. C. and W. E. Lambert (1972*) Attitudes and motivation in second-language learning.* Rowley, Mass: Newbury House.

Harris, V. (1998). 'Making boys make progress'. *Language Learning Journal,* **18**, 56–62.

Heafford, M. (1990) Teachers may teach but do learners learn? *Language Learning Journal* **1** March, 88–9

Hodgkin, R. (1998) *Partnership with pupils.* Children UK, Summer.

Lee, J. Buckland, D. and Shaw, G. (1998) *The invisible child.* CILT.

Levin, B. (1995) 'Improving educational productivity through a focus on learners', *International Studies in Educational Administration,* **60**, 15–21.

Maccoby, E. and Jacklin, G. (1975) *The psychology of sex differences.* Stanford University Press.

Mercer, N. (1994) 'Neo-Vygotskian Theory and Classroom Education'. In: Steirer, B. and Maybin, J. (eds) *Language, Literacy and Learning in Educational Practice.* Multilingual Matters Ltd in association with the Open University: 96.

Mifsud, C. (1993). 'Gender differentials in the classroom'. *Research in Education,* **49,** 11–12.

Nieto, S. (1994) 'Lessons from students on creating a chance to dream'. *Harvard Educational Review,* **64,** 4, 392–426.

O'Malley, J. M. and Chamot, A. U. (1990) *Learning strategies in second language acquisition.* Cambridge University Press.

Phelan, P., Davidson, A. L. and Cao, H. (1992) *Speaking up: students' perspectives on school.* Phi, Delta: Kappan, **73,** 9, 695–704.

Powell, B. and Batters, J. (1986). 'Sex of teacher and the image of foreign languages in schools'. *Educational Studies,* **12,** 245–254.

Rubin, J. (1975) 'What the "good language learner" can teach us'. *TESOL Quarterly,* **9,** 41–51.

Rudduck, J. (1996) *Student voices: what can they tell us as partners in change* paper given at the BEMAS, Annual Conference, Cambridge, March.

Rudduck, J. (1999) 'Teacher practice and the student voice'. In: Lang M., Olson J., Hansen H. and Bunder W. (eds) *Changing schools/changing practices: perspectives on educational reform and teacher professionalism.* Louvain: Graant 41–54.

Rudduck, J., Chaplain, R. and Wallace, G. (1996) *School improvement: what can pupils tell us.* David Fulton.

Soo Hoo, S. (1993) 'Students as partners in research and restructuring schools'. *The Educational Forum,* **57,** Summer, 386–393.

Spender, D. (1982). *Invisible woman: the schooling scandal.* Writers and Readers.

Stern, H. H. (1975) 'What can we find from the good language learner?'. *Canadian Modern Language Review,* **31,** 304–318.

Vygotsky, L. (1962) *Thought and language.* Cambridge, MA: MIT Press.

Warrington, M., Younger, M. and Williams, J. (2000) 'Student attitudes and the gender gap'. *British Educational Research Journal,* **26,** 3, 393–407.

Appendices

APPENDIX A

INSET or DEPARTMENTAL DISCUSSION DOCUMENT

This has been used in schools to focus discussion on the report. The findings from the project are grouped under headings which relate to the previous chapters. What the pupils say is summarised in sections A.1 – A.3 and the perceptions of their teachers in A.4.

A.1   **The distinctive nature of Modern Foreign Languages**

A.1.1   **Particular characteristics of MFL**

Individual pupils focus on particular concerns, but, across cohorts, a general picture emerges of pupils' perspectives which relate to their understanding of the distinctive nature of MFL and the problems that this may present to them as learners in school. This has to do with the following factors:

A.1.1.1 Organisational frameworks:

the National Curriculum and GCSE impose

- four discrete skill areas listening, reading, writing and speaking;
- need for accuracy.

MFL is seen as cumulative acquisition of non-negotiable linguistic information.

A.1.1.2 Obligations on pupils to:

- learn the language structures;
- use these to interact with MFL speakers;
- make them part of their behavioural repertoire;

A.1.1.3 Classroom activity which is more complex than that in other subjects and which poses particular challenges because:

- its content is both subject matter and the language itself;

- the language is broken down into independent skills – listening, reading; speaking, writing – each with specific demands;

- its language skills are interrelated and complex;

- there is grammar content which is rule-based and must be learnt;

- one language has a particular system and structure which is different from another: learning a second foreign language (L3) in the perceptions of the pupils interviewed does not always benefit from learning a first foreign language (L2);

- a standard model of the MFL is generally presented in school which may not correspond to the MFL encountered in the country;

- all lexis is new;

- proficiency in MFL is cumulative, developmental and requires perseverance

- the provisionality of MFL language acquisition makes demands on long term memory;

- proficiency requires continuous practice and higher level cognitive skills;

- a considerable amount of information has to be acquired; progression is not fixed;

- sound literacy skills in L1 are necessary for good performance;

- rewards in the classroom are more likely to be for accuracy rather than for ideas: differences of sophistication between L1 and L2/3 may be frustrating;

- MFL learning makes particular demands on individual pupils to establish working practices upon which successful performance is dependent;

- learning an MFL requires pupils to be organised and systematic, and able to refer back to notes and rules;

- learners have to take responsibility for learning outcomes and to work independently;

- teaching an MFL lends itself to particular teaching styles and different classroom relationships.

A.1.2   **Communicative competence**

The communicative aspect of MFL learning poses further personal and psychological challenges:

- Pupils have to speak clearly and in public.

- Emotional considerations may impinge on a learner's confidence.

- Communicating with native speakers of the MFL and developing empathy requires particular skills and commitment.

- Cultural awareness is important for effective communicative competence.

- Positive experience abroad may contribute to and reinforce successful. performance and motivation, but linguistic 'surprises' may occur in the foreign context.

- Most pupils have to operate within an unfamiliar cultural frame.

- All learners are entirely dependent on the teacher for knowledge of the MFL and on the teacher's skill to impart enthusiasm for, and expertise in the MFL.

- Teachers must do this within prescribed methodological and structural requirements imposed by the National Curriculum and GCSE syllabi and must use the target language as the main teaching medium.

- These requirements may distance pupils from relating MFL to its local context and to their needs.

A.1.3 The second (or third) foreign language

- Learning a second MFL (L3) can be a very different experience from the first MFL (L2).

- The complexity of learning one foreign language may be compounded by learning another one.

- L3 may interfere with L2.

- L2 may be preferred to L3 or vice versa because of the nature of the tasks or the content.

- One MFL may be perceived as being more difficult or less interesting than another language.

- If two languages are learnt there may be differences in teacher style and relationships.

- The L2 may form part of the active language repertoire and social experience of individuals outside school whereas L3 may not have the same status.

- Motivation and application to L2 and L3 in school may differ.

- Negative attitudes towards the country where L2/L3 is spoken may also impact on pupil performance.

However, pupils exposed to a range of languages outside school may develop learning strategies that can be constructively implemented in learning L2/L3 school languages.

A.1.4 Other factors that are critical for MFL

- seating arrangements and their impact on MFL specific activities

Other organisational factors are critical but may not be exclusive to MFL. These include:

- class size;
- the potential for individual monitoring and attention;
- seating arrangements and working partnerships;
- gender balance;
- gendered working practices of the group.

A.2 Classroom interaction and interpersonal relationships

A.2.1 The relationship between the teacher and the learners is, perhaps, more significant than in other subjects:

- Teaching an MFL imposes interactive and communicative demands.

- The teacher has both to function as a model for the target language as well as to encourage pupils to empathise with the target language community and its cultural context.

- MFL requires an equal emphasis on four discrete language skill areas – listening, reading, writing and speaking, each requiring different relationships with and between pupils, and different dynamics.

A.2.2 Additionally and more generally:

- Teacher–pupil relationships are influenced by the rigours and pressures imposed by the National Curriculum for MFL and GCSE syllabi and examinations.

- Learning an MFL in school does not always appear to relate to using the MFL in a real context so relationships are sometimes based on artificial situations.

- The MFL teacher has also to monitor, diagnose and target pupil progress individually and collectively to enable pupils to perform accurately and effectively.

- Teachers rarely allow pupils to reach their own understandings in an exploratory way by using English as a means of communication.

- The process, focus and language are different, so different relationships are encouraged and ensue.

A.2.3   **Key issues relating to classroom relationships in Years 9 and Year 11 emerging from the data are:**

- In MFL pupils recognise that they are particularly dependent on their teacher: for the language they are to learn and use, and for good management, clear lesson structure and careful organisation of tasks so that they can learn efficiently.

- Teachers, in the opinion of the pupils, need to be competent, enthusiastic users of the target language and able to promote independent and successful learning.

- Pupils know what a 'good teacher' is: they have clear perceptions and expectations based on their understanding and experiences of MFL classrooms. He or she:

  – has a good rapport with the class;

  – listens to and understands individual pupils;

  – creates positive working relationships based on mutual respect;

  – ensures learning takes place.

- Teacher gender is irrelevant; it is the teacher-pupil relationship which matters.

- Boys respect management that is consistent, firm and fair.

- Boys respond well to skilful managers with additional personal qualities that engage and motivate; being happy, well informed and able to create a relaxed atmosphere promotes learning as well as interesting content.

- Boys who feel comfortable in class and at ease with the language want to take part.

- Classroom interaction is likely to be successful if management and relationships are predictable.

A.2.4   **However, relationships are variable and some boys may be particularly sensitive to the learning environment that obtains:**

- A breakdown in effective communication can impact negatively on performance.

- Boys do not respond well when some pupils are treated differently from others: boys want relationships that are consistent and stable, where all pupils are treated as equals.

A.2.5   **Most boys claim that they engage differently with the learning environment in MFL than girls:**

- when the work is boring boys tend to switch off; 'girls just do it anyway';

- boys confirm that, in language lessons, they are:

  – less likely than girls to adopt and maintain the sound study skills, good presentation and thorough learning strategies demanded of them in MFL;

  – less inclined to concentrate, memorise, listen to others, follow instructions and work constructively with peers;

– more reliant on the teacher to motivate them to communicate and interact in the target language.

| A.2.6 | **Boys' attitudes affect relations in class:** |

- Boys see their willingness to work as being dependent on good relations in class, on the teacher's attitude to them and on his or her teaching style.

- Boys, in particular, respond well to humour, variety and fun.

- Boys suggest that motivation and feelings of success are mediated through relations in class with a key factor being the teacher's concern about their progress.

| A.2.7 | **Attitudes, however, change when working relationships break down:** |

- Some pupils resent the disruptive behaviour of others.

- Negative attitudes are reinforced and develop over time, with serious consequences in Year 11.

- Performance in class is affected by unpredictable factors which have consequences on pupil attitude; these may be both provisional and variable.

- Some disillusioned boys recognise and can identify strategies to improve but see no need to succeed.

- However, specific, regularly assessed targets can positively affect the attitudes of learners, especially younger boys.

- An element of language choice for Subject Options can enhance the positive attitudes of some boys; this may foster better relationships within the group.

| A.2.8 | **Boys perceive that MFL lessons are especially complex and can lead to tensions in relationships:** |

- Some boys were particularly anxious for teachers to maintain personal relationships and pay particular attention to them as individuals.

- Boys respond positively to explanations when these are interactive, and to the challenge of a lively pace.

- Boys identify certain pedagogic practices in MFL which can lead to disaffection, boredom and poor behaviour.

| A.2.9 | **Boys' relationships through talk:** |

- Speaking and talking are sometimes ambiguously interpreted in MFL.

- Talking in MFL lessons for examination practice is seen as an unnatural use of language in what may be an ambiguous social setting.

- For some boys their teacher's use of the target language as the medium of classroom interaction is seen as self evident, natural and beneficial for their learning; for others, lack of comprehension can cause problems.

- Communicating with others abroad can enhance motivation, especially for younger boys.

- The success of pupil-to-pupil talk seems to rely on friendly, collaborative partnerships rather than competitive ones.

- Group work and working in mixed gender groups are seen as less successful ways of working.

A.2.10	**The impact of gender on relationships in class:**

- The gender balance in a class often affects relationships.

- Boys' and girls' behaviour, relationships and working practices differ which may lead teachers to treat them differently.

- Learners appear to believe that success in MFL is not dependent on gender – boys, however, may sometimes go about it in different ways from girls.

- Boys and girls respond in a number of ways to public performance, such as role plays or pupil directed activity in front of the class – this can change the atmosphere in an MFL lesson.

A.2.11	**Which boys underperform, what are the relationships that obtain and how does underperformance develop?**

- Identifying individual underperformers can sometimes be problematic; there may be tensions between teachers' assumptions and pupils' perceptions.

- The data reveal that boys of all abilities may underperform in MFL.

- Boys' poor performance can result in a **downward spiral** which is increasingly difficult to correct. This may lead to low co-operation and low motivation and can create discipline problems in class.

- Underperformance is the result of a range of complex factors caused by particular events which may differ for each pupil.

- Particular to MFL is that understanding and progress is cumulative so pupils in difficulty quickly get lost and find it increasingly difficult to get back on track.

A.2.12	**Teachers, then, should, in boys' opinion:**

- be aware of individual pupil needs and focus on the positive, so that they can provide reassurance and show understanding, as well as get everyone involved;

- be dynamic in order to manage and foster talk confidently;

- try to devise MFL activities that are fun, varied and flexible so that pupils are motivated and focused on the task;

- use the target language sensitively to ensure that there is meaningful linguistic progression and, by explaining tasks clearly, help pupils understand what they have to do and why, in language learning terms, they are doing them;

- provide individual guidance, clear parameters and targets;

- be fair yet firm;

- set realistic tasks;

- have realisable yet challenging expectations;

- involve the pupils in learning decisions;

- set tasks where the pupils are likely to make few mistakes;

- encourage work with a partner of their choice where they can express themselves as individuals;

- monitor progress closely, keeping pupils on track before they get lost and then left behind;

- ensure seating arrangements which allow pupils to get on with others and which respond to how each pupil defines the work in social or productive terms.

A.2.13   **Progress is not only dependent on the teacher, it is also dependent on the pupil. Pupils should therefore:**

- take a proactive stance by taking responsibility for their learning and making efforts to improve;

- concentrate particularly on the beginnings of lessons when a language model is being presented;

- make known any lack of understanding and seek help;

- negotiate strategies with the teacher early on, to catch up on lost ground.

A.2.14   **If such strategies and procedures are not in place underperformance is likely to be a self-fulfilling prophecy:**

> … maybe if I was good at it I would put in more effort … but I'm not good at it and it just doesn't bother me. HJB9:9

A.3   **Boys' awareness of what helps and what hinders their learning**

A willingness to work is relatively precarious especially when the tasks and activities are seen as difficult. It would appear that:

A.3.1   **Motivation is dependent on self analysis by pupils and teachers: negative motivation leads to failure, to pupils blaming the teacher for underperformance and to pupils not taking responsibility for their own learning. It also leads, with negatively motivated, underperforming pupils, to teachers adopting coping strategies.**

A.3.2   **The relative difficulty of one kind of activity may be lessened if the working atmosphere is positive, if the teacher is firm, if there are clear parameters of work and behaviour, and if the rapport between the teacher and the class is supportive.**

A.3.3   **Boys believe they are likely to perform better if there is:**

- a feeling of ownership of content, task and strategy;

- an element of fun;

- humour: the use of humour by the teacher and in his or her responses to the pupils;

- a learning challenge;

- a development of thinking skills, especially in terms of teacher explanation: grammar, for example, being made explicit;

- active learning: where they move around, and, especially in Year 9, make things like posters and displays;

- purposefulness and transparency: performance is improved when the teacher's purposes are explicit and clear, and the aims of lessons as well as lesson procedures are understood.

A.3.4   **Boys say they learn more efficiently if:**

- the mode of working, collaborative or independent, is one they find helpful;

- the activities they are given are realistic, achievable, enjoyable, unthreatening and within their control;

- they are in a positive working mood;

- they understand for each skill area which strategies they need to adopt and why these help;

- they can find and experience an instrumental and/or integrative motivation in what they are doing.

A.3.5   **Motivation may be enhanced, in Year 9, by real situations like going to the country, meeting people and by contacts with others; in Year 11 by having wider goals such as a good grade in GCSE.**

A.3.6   **Motivation may be decreased by:**

- making too many mistakes;
- not seeing the point;
- boredom;
- repetitive tasks;
- copying;
- unclear tasks and activities;
- unclear, fuzzy or fast audio recordings.

It is clear that boys, identified by their teachers as underperforming, are able to recognise and describe strategies and activities which would help them. This level of awareness seems general whatever the ability of the class. There appear to be boys who underperform, who may be unprepared, at times, to help themselves as much as they know they should but who, nonetheless, find something positive about their language learning. There are other boys identified as underperformers who view language learning more negatively and who are much less willing to take responsibility for their learning and its improvement. Underperformance is thus exacerbated by those who may be positive about some aspects of learning an MFL being in the same class as those who are not. This poses problems of management for the teacher especially when the pupils see it as the teacher's function to create an atmosphere in which all pupils can have opportunities to learn. They also realise that poor relationships with each other as well as the relationships they have with the teacher may decrease their chances of success if negatively motivated boys dominate.

A.4   **Teachers' reflections on boys and modern foreign languages**

A.4.1   **Awareness of the problem of boys' underachievement in MFL**

Among the teachers interviewed there was:

- a widespread assumption that girls are likely to do better than boys;
- an acceptance that gender makes a difference;
- a view that boys are less mature than girls, so are less focused;
- a readiness to address the problem.

Teachers were clearly able to identify aspects of their usual teaching style that might appeal more or less to boys and girls:

- An insistence on the expectation of high standards among all pupils.

A.4.2   **Teachers' understanding of the learning needs of boys**

If the needs of boys are to be met in MFL classes then there should be:

- variety of activity in the classroom such as:
  - whole class directed work by the teacher;
  - role play;
  - group work (not so often);
  - focused reading activities;
  - listening to recordings as a whole class;
  - listening to cassettes individually;
  - using worksheets;
  - watching videos;
  - using ICT;
  - writing (although boys can respond negatively to this).

- pace
  - to keep disenchantment at bay;
  - to hustle boys into action.

- physical activity
  boys need to:
  - move round the classroom;
  - take part in a game;
  - engage in miming activities;
  - come forward to write on the board.

- competition
  boys respond to:
  - active participation;
  - competitions and competitive games;
  - challenges.

- a teacher with a sense of fun

- explanations of grammar and how the language works:
  - more able boys are not easily satisfied by learning set-piece phrases;
  - to be done in English.

- a clear understanding of the purpose of the activity

A.4.3   **Target setting**

Target setting is a means of focusing attention and increasing motivation.

A.4.4   **Teachers' awareness of the pupils' dependence on the teacher in MFL and of the importance of interpersonal relationships**

- In other subjects there is an external corpus of knowledge which teachers are helping pupils to understand; in MFL it is the interaction between teachers and pupils which is the medium of learning.

- The essence of teaching a foreign language can become a barrier to the development of a good working relationships, particularly when the teaching is conducted in the target language.

- Pupil dependence is apparent in relation to the setting and completion of tasks.

- Boys who 'muck about' can be a barrier to effective learning.

- A teacher who sustains a good relationship with a group of difficult boys can get a very positive response.

- Achieving a good working relationship is dependant on the qualities and character of the teacher:
  - strictness with a human dimension
  - interest in pupils as individuals and available at the end of lessons and outside lessons
  - the 'strict teacher' and the 'ready to have a laugh' teacher

- Good relationships depend on teachers having a structured behaviour management policy so that they:
  - apply the same rules;
  - insist that homework is being done;
  - carry out the detention regime fairly and consistently;
  - expect tenacity and rigour in the work of both teachers and pupils.

A.4.5   Teachers' awareness of the link between motivation and success for boys

- There is a need to motivate pupils to learn particularly in MFL where the subject is perceived by pupils to be 'hard'; this can be helped by:

  - study visits or exchanges;
  - supportive parents with a positive attitude to MFL learning;
  - opportunities for pupils to meet native speakers of a language;
  - MFL having the same status as numeracy and literacy;
  - male role models;
  - topics to capture the interests of boys, for example, leisure activities or relating to future job opportunities;
  - boys always seeing the point of what they are doing.

- Boys' motivation may be influenced by:

  - seating; where and with whom they sit;
  - group work which may not lead to effective learning.

A.4.6   Teachers' perception of the inherent and distinctive difficulty for many boys in learning MFL

- Boys' less reliable progress in MFL may be caused by:
  - their perceived social immaturity;
  - their intolerance of what they see as irrelevant subject matter;
  - the intrinsic difficulty of making tangible progress;
  - their inability to sustain attention;
  - their unwillingness to engage in situations where they think they may fail.

- Teachers recognise that language learning is just not easy:
  - it imposes a constant demand to look at detail;
  - there is little working for any length of time with a partner;
  - it is composed of many little tasks where pupils always need help.

- The very nature of MFL is:
  - inherently more attractive to girls than to boys.

APPENDIX B

WHAT MAKES GOOD QUALITY TEACHING AND LEARNING? – A QUESTIONNAIRE

In his teaching practice school in Bedfordshire Stéphane Muller, a student on the 2000–2001 European Teacher Programme (which leads to the joint award of PGCE/Maîtrise: Français Langue Étrangère), at Homerton College, Cambridge wanted to investigate the attitude of his Year 10 class to learning French. His intention was to use the results of a survey to help adapt activities for boys. He devised a questionnaire (below) based on ten statements taken from the report. His respondents were asked to:

1. put the statements into rank order, 1 being most important, 10 being least important;

2. justify each statement with a short comment.

QUESTIONNAIRE

What makes good quality teaching and learning in French?

Read carefully the ten sentences below. Classify them with numbers 1–10, answering the question: What is the most important thing for you in a French class? (1 being most important, 10 being least important). Justify each answer with a short comment.

a   a logical sequence of activities

b   interest in the learning activities

c   awareness of the learning objectives

d   learning objectives translated into clear targets

e   tasks well matched to your ability

f   tasks which are challenging but achievable

g   a real purpose to the activities

h   responsibility for your learning with an element of choice

i   assessment informs future development and monitors your progress

j   feedback which is frequent and constructive and which provides further learning targets

---

Stéphane's students rated most highly:
- interest in the learning activities
- tasks which are challenging but achievable
- a real purpose to the activities

As he commented, the findings were not altogether surprising. However, when he planned lessons with these three considerations in mind he noticed an improvement in attitude. What was perhaps of even greater interest than the numerical rank ordering were the comments which the pupils made after the statements, for example:

- responsibility for your learning with an element of choice

  – *yes, but too much choice can be confusing and not all pupils are sufficiently confident to take responsibility for learning*   *10*

  – *I prefer being told what to do – set targets etc*   *10*

– *being told makes you more focussed*	*9*
– *must be free to investigate subjects you are personally interested in*	*5*
– *not necessary – the teacher knows best how much and what you should learn*	*9*

- tasks which are challenging but achievable

– *a challenge is important for improvement/testing the brain*	*2*
– *this improves learning but very hard tasks are not good*	*5*
– *if tasks aren't challenging progression is too slow*	*1*
– *accelerates learning when challenged, but not overwhelmed*	*2*
– *creates a sense of achievement and increases confidence*	*1*

This is only a glimpse at some very revealing pupil attitudes. Other student-teachers on the current, 2000–2001, European Teacher Programme are in the process of running the questionnaire with different groups to explore its potential in discovering more about those whom we teach. Perhaps an MFL department would like to do the same.

APPENDIX C

EXTRACTS FROM A LITERATURE REVIEW

Early on in the project a review of the literature was undertaken for the QCA by Dr Helen Demetriou. Here we present a summary only, with the material re-organised under topics that emerged as centrally important in the data from the present study; these topics are discussed in the body of the report. It should be noted that these were written in 1999; the finite duration of the project has prevented them from being updated.

Overall, the data from the present study confirm much of the general picture emerging from earlier studies. However, the report highlights, because of the emphasis on pupil perspectives in the data gathering, the usefulness of listening to what the pupils have to say about teaching and learning.

C1   **What a review of the literature tells us**

C.1.1   **Gender related issues: boys and Modern Foreign Languages**

As early as 1693, Locke's educational treatise addressed boys' underachievement in their mastery of Latin in which he noted that girls learned French rapidly and successfully using the conversational method he advocated. An example of the striking indication of gender bias towards foreign languages was Beswick's (1976) observation of 250 boys who took French when they entered his school, none took French at sixth form. In reviewing the evidence for the gulf between the sexes in languages, it is important to consider *'factors such as intelligence, aptitude and memory ... parental support, socio-economic grouping and teacher-pupil interaction'* (Powell and Batters, 1985).

C.1.2   **Attitude and motivation**

In general, girls and boys differ quite distinctly in the attitudes and enthusiasm they bring to the language lesson. In particular, girls have been shown to be more positive towards French (Burstall, Jamieson, Cohen and Hargreaves, 1974). In an attitude survey of 953 pupils at the beginning of their second year of French or German in six mixed comprehensive schools, girls expressed more positive opinions of foreign languages and were generally more accepting of the necessity to learn foreign languages than boys (Powell and Batters, 1985). When 7- to 10-year-old boys were asked why they thought girls did better at modern languages than boys, poor attitude emerged as the key factor: *'[we] don't take it seriously'* (Harris, 1998, p57). Furthermore, Lee, Buckland and Shaw (1998) examined the attitudes and experiences of Year 9 average ability girls and boys towards modern foreign languages and found that girls spent more available time actually focusing on the work they were given, and were more willing to try to understand and follow the instructions they were given while boys were less inclined to do so.

C.1.3   **Learning strategies and styles**

It is generally accepted that girls' compliant, methodical, and motivated approaches to learning contrast sharply with the instant, short-term working habits of boys (e.g. Moore, 1996). Beswick (1976) found that girls were more prepared to undertake more painstaking work and attributed this trait to their earlier maturity allied with greater social awareness, compared with boys' vocal inhibitions and self-consciousness. Boys' reasons for dropping French would typically be that it involved 'too much hard work' and 'tedious learning processes'. In contrast, girls respond to a lack of success by feelings of anxiety that lead them to work harder, and they will even resort to rote learning of vocabulary and grammar (Graham and Rees, 1995). Boys 'don't take the same amount of pride' in work of this nature (Clark and Trafford, 1996, p12) and instead prefer being left to their own devices – a rare feature of the modern language classroom. A series of interviews revealed that boys reflected a general concern about the lack of independence offered in modern languages classrooms compared to maths or physics where they are required more often to work things out for themselves (Harris, 1998).

C.1.4   Reading skills

Differences in the quality and quantity of reading materials and reading levels between girls and boys might provide clues for differences in their modern foreign language performance. Findings by Sammons (1995) revealed that over a nine-year period of study, the reading skills of girls were more advanced than those of boys. Moreover, Whitehead et al. (1977) found that the choice of preferred reading material between girls and boys differed greatly. Whereas girls' favourite stories involved human relationships, impulses, feelings and moral valuations, boys preferred adventures where self-assertion and power were prominent. Recreational reading was not a favourite pastime of adolescent boys, so that by 14 years, 40% of boys were choosing not to read books. Rather, 30% more girls than boys of this age group were reading narrative fiction and 10% of boys by age 14 read only factual and informative texts. An OFSTED (1993) report highlighted boys' literacy skills as contributing to poor performance in English. It found that boys have narrower experiences of fiction, write more predictably, have difficulty with the affective aspects of English, place less emphasis in understanding character, and scan for relevant information rather than read from beginning to end. Moreover, boys have been described as 'reluctant to learn and especially to read' (Downes, 1998, p15). Regarding reading in the language classroom in particular, Bugel and Buunk (1996) have emphasised the importance of readers' likes and dislikes when they confront a text.

C.1.5   Oral skills

In a study by Stables and Stables (1996) in which they assessed students' perceptions of the way they chose A level subjects, French was the third most commonly chosen subject by girls and the eighth among boys. Specifically, speaking the language was the most popular reason given by students (both girls and boys) for their enjoyment of the subject.

Much research on language and gender has focused on the differences between male and female speech ability (e.g. Trudgill, 1974). Oral ability plays a central role in language learning. One explanation for the gap between the sexes is that boys are often reluctant to speak in public (Powell and Littlewood, 1982). Boys are known to experience more difficulty when talking about their feelings, they are less likely to develop stories through their play and they use fewer words in their play. By adolescence, the all-important self-image curtails much conversation because of boys' fear of frustration at appearing tongue-tied (Politzer, 1983; Tannen, 1995). Added to this, they feel inhibited when they attempt to produce unusual sounds in the presence of girls (Burstall et al, 1974). Moreover, boys enjoy the creative and imaginative element of learning where there is a greater degree of independence from the teacher, and in so doing may be less willing to perform the repetitive oral tasks required of the language lesson (Powell, 1986). However, these findings are not conclusive as other researchers have shown instead that in fact boys enjoy taking the floor (Clark and Trafford, 1996). A survey by Barton (1997) evaluated the learning preferences of 288 Year 8 pupils and showed that speaking was the most popular core skill with boys, while writing was most enjoyed by girls. These results are more in line with those findings of boys' poorer listening and reading skills which make talking-based activities more desirable (Aplin, 1991; Batters, 1986; Graham and Rees, 1995).

C.1.6   Socio-cultural pressures

More evidence is accumulating from cross-cultural studies to suggest that differences in subject perceptions are in fact linked to attitudes within particular societies, rather than sex differences in ability being innate (Klainin, Fensham and West, 1989; Loulidi, 1990). The gender differences in attitude towards modern language learning may stem from social, cultural and parental pressures which portray language ability as admirable for girls, but unmanly for boys. Indeed, ' ... *powerful forces are at play in our culture which shape the attitudes towards learning, literacy and behaviour among boys and young men*' (QCA, 1998, p5).

A study by Beswick (1976) that analysed teacher reports found that boys seemed to underachieve in relation to girls. A *'strong social pressure towards science for boys, which removed the motivation from language study'* (p36) was the reason given. The more positive attitudes that emanate from girls could also be a consequence of the fact that they have more positive attitudes towards foreigners than boys do; boys have been shown instead to be more ethnocentric. Moreover, by adolescence, this ethnocentricity among boys intensifies as their self-confidence decreases and the need to identify with their peers increases (Phillips and Filmer-Sankey, 1993). Peers are of course an important influence for children in the school years and generally boys gain little credibility among their peers for working hard or for being successful (QCA, 1998). The influence of parents should also be considered where role-models are established in connection with certain subjects. For example, there is tendency for mothers to help with English homework and fathers with maths (Arnot, 1982). Moreover, middle class parents seem to encourage boys to pursue physical sciences and girls foreign languages (Riddell, 1992).

C.2   The distinctive nature of Modern Foreign Languages

Studies have found that pupils are not influenced by a feminine image of the subject. For example, interviews by Barton (1997) with a small number of pupils from Years 8, 9 and 10 revealed that, while boys attached more importance to other subjects such as maths and science, their motivation in languages was not affected by any notions of it being a girls' subject.

Reynolds (1995) found that for English teaching, the use of drama techniques such as role-play are effective measures for boys. Place (1997) also highlighted the importance of speaking practice within the classroom. Her strategy was to set homework in form of speaking to be recorded on pupils' individual cassettes, beginning with a couple of open-ended questions. She found this to be a refreshing change and engaging task for the pupils instead of using their exercise books. They valued the 'personal touch' that this type of learning strategy brought with it. This technique moreover contributed to the development of self-confidence in the speaking skills of the pupils. Other researchers have observed that females use social communication strategies more than males, and have suggested that boys might benefit from using 'filler' phrases (*bof, eh bien*) (Halliwell and Jones, 1991) that give them time to think; and all-purpose words (*le truc*) that help maintain the flow of conversation (Politzer, 1983).

Attempts have been made to differentiate between different modern languages, and children's views of them. Pupils' attitudes towards French, German and Spanish as subjects at various stages of their learning were explored and the study showed that pupils in Key Stage 3 were at least as positive in their attitudes towards German and Spanish as they were towards French. In particular, boys were more positively motivated when offered German or Spanish as FL1. This finding was attributed to the fact that German, for example, has a more masculine image (Phillips and Filmer-Sankey, 1993). Evidence has shown that German is perceived as a much more difficult language than French (Pritchard, 1987). In general, gender differences in responses to 'failure' may relate to attribution theory (Dickinson, 1995). Whereas girls feel in control of learning and recognise what they need to do in order to make progress, some boys feel it is out of their hands, attributing their lack of success to the task: *'it's boring'*, *'a waste of time'*, or to their ability: *'I'm no good at French'*. Researchers have hypothesised that the first stages of learning German are easier than French because of its similarity with English. The similarity and familiarity of German with English is an example of why certain languages may be more acceptable to boys. Furthermore, the guttural pronunciation required of German may be better suited to boys when the voice is breaking as this process can exacerbate the difficulties experienced with the more delicate French language (Phillips and Filmer-Sankey, 1993).

C.3   Interpersonal relationships and dependency on the teacher

C.3.1   Teaching strategies and styles

The differences in learning styles of girls and boys make it necessary for teachers to use appropriate strategies. It has been noted for example, that *'the conventional reluctance of teachers to introduce written equivalents of spoken passages and dialogues too soon in learning sequences might be having a negative effect on boys' progress'* (Powell, 1979).

Teachers often display different attitudes to behaviour depending on the gender of the pupil, and consequently, the quality and quantity of attention given can be quite different for girls and boys. For example, boys are more likely to receive harsher and more negative comments in general than those directed at girls guilty of the same offences (Jackson and Lahadenne, 1971). During an investigation of subject preferences and choices of 1,204 pupils in 19 secondary schools, Ormerod (1975) commented that *'in the co-educational class the teacher may unwittingly adopt practices which encourage the boys, while reinforcing the girls' belief that physical science is a male preserve'*. Whereas teachers tend to participate in boys' play, their interactions with girls are more verbal. It has also been noted that although boys receive two-thirds of the teacher's attention in class, much of this attention is negative and reflects disciplinary problems (Spender, 1982). Moreover, an OFSTED (1993) report on English showed that boys receive less overt praise: they are more likely to be given encouragement on an individual basis, possibly as a result of teachers' appreciation that it is not always 'cool' for boys to be praised in class.

Alternatively, some researchers have shown that there are more similarities than differences in teaching styles, and that teachers respond to their pupils' behaviour rather than to their gender (Mifsud, 1993; Powell and Batters, 1986; Wilkinson and Marrett, 1985). However, Powell and Batters (1986) found that 86.6% of pupils at the end of their 3rd year saw languages neither as boys' nor girls' subjects, compared with 42% of teachers who felt that pupils do see languages as being more appropriate for females.

C.3.2   Single-sex and mixed-sex groupings

Aware of the findings that boys often feel tongue-tied in the language classroom (Politzer, 1983), researchers set out to compare differences in pupils', and particularly boys', language learning achievements in the single-sex versus the mixed-sex classroom. For example, a significant finding by Burstall et al (1974) revealed that 70% of the boys in single-sex schools enjoyed learning French, compared with 49% in co-educational schools. A study by Beswick (1976) targeted seven boys' schools (three comprehensives, two LEA grammar schools, and two small independent schools); and eight mixed schools (six comprehensives and two small grammar schools). The schools were asked to give information about entries of boys and girls for public examinations in French. Fewer co-educational boys took French through to A level. Of the boys' schools, 10.4% took French, and 11.8% of their sixth year were taking A level French. The comparative figures for the co-educational schools were 5.6% and 4.7%. In the mixed schools, more girls were taking O level and A level French, and boys' attainment in the co-educational schools was lower than that of the girls. Moreover, boys in single-sex schools did better than boys in mixed schools, and by 15 years, this difference was statistically significant for all social classes.

A study that targeted single-sex teaching groups in French within a mixed school found that boys improved in their second year compared to the previous year in mixed classes. In addition, girls benefited academically from being segregated: *'I felt embarrassed speaking French in front of the boys. Now I do better and show more interest because we are all girls'* (16-year-old girl) (Beswick, 1976). Furthermore, in a study that described marked improvement, especially by boys, when pupils were segregated by gender, Powell (1979) highlighted the importance of setting according to sex as being *'beneficial at least on the basis of increased positive attitudes to foreign language learning by both sexes'* (p23). More recent findings confirm the importance of single-sex classes for boys' learning. For example, boys at a mixed comprehensive school recorded large improvements in their academic performance after being split into single-sex classes to counter the 'disadvantages' of being taught with girls. A girl who believed there were also benefits for girls commented: *'As soon as we were separated, there was a completely different atmosphere'* (Syal and Trump, 1996). Moreover, a study by Cheng, Payne and Witherspoon (1995) who monitored MFL uptake found 23% of boys from boy-only schools, 28% of girls from girl-only schools, 8% of boys from mixed schools and 25% of girls from mixed schools chose languages at A level.

| C.3.3 | **The influence of the gender of the teacher** |

In a study that aimed to ascertain pupils' perceptions of English, boys perceived it as a girls' subject, due mainly to the fact that it is taught mainly by women (Wheatley, 1996). In language departments also, researchers have expressed concern over the predominance of women teachers (Powell, 1986; Pritchard, 1987). Of particular concern is that it is *'likely to reinforce the male perception that languages are a girls' subject',* which contribute to the perpetuation of a *vicious circle resulting in boys'* underachievement in languages' (Pritchard, 1987). Indeed, *'It is interesting to note the very much higher proportion of women than men teaching foreign languages. This may be held to reinforce the belief that foreign languages are more popular with girls than boys because they are most often taught by women'* (APU, 1985). However, this same survey found that pupils were relatively unaware of the gender bias and did not feel it made a significant difference to their perception of the subject, feeling instead that the personality of the teacher was more important than their gender (Clark and Trafford, 1994). Subsequent findings from a study that addressed differences in attitudes between girls and boys after five years of modern language study through interviews with 75 students, twelve language teachers and two head teachers, highlighted the significance of teacher personality and classroom practice from student interviews (Clark and Trafford, 1995).

Similar results were found in a study involving single-sex and co-educational schools where the relationship between a liking for the teacher and subject preference, but not necessarily subject choice was apparent (Ormerod, 1975). Moreover, Powell and Batters (1985) did not find significant results in their investigation of questions relating to the gender of the modern language teacher. They concluded by saying: *'It would be foolhardy to suggest that the predominance of female teachers in language departments increases the so-called 'femininity' of the subject, but that pattern is part of wider social sex-stereotyping of roles which is bound to influence a child's view of the world'.* In fact a follow-up study indicated that pupils preferred female teachers because this contributed to overall perception of languages as easy, non-serious subjects (Powell and Batters, 1986).

| C.4 | **Boys' awareness of their pedagogic needs** |

In the 1960s, several researchers highlighted the importance of the incorporation of teaching aids and activities in the classroom in order to increase pupils' interest in language learning. Since then, studies have pinpointed the challenge of communication and in particular the flexibility in pace or content that contributes to a positive image of foreign languages. For example, studies have identified the need for tailoring teacher behaviour to students' declared desires. In particular these have advocated the adoption of humanistic and co-operative approaches between teacher and student as helping to improve the image of foreign language study, as well as noting that the language teacher's relationship with the pupil's family can influence foreign language enrolment. More recent evidence has shown that offering boys greater choice over what they learn may help address their underachievement in modern languages, but they may not profit from this unless they are given explicit guidelines regarding how to go about their learning (Harris, 1998).

Traditionally, boys have chosen to pursue mathematics and the sciences, believing that these subjects have greater potential for career choices. Beswick (1976) confirmed this finding when boys regarded modern foreign languages as having 'poor career prospects'. More recently, however, research has shown that despite the difficulties experienced by boys in learning languages, they are beginning to appreciate their increasing significance for future careers. For example, even at the difficult stages of language learning, boys still viewed German as more useful than French or Spanish and boys viewed German as particularly useful in industry and commerce (Phillips and Filmer-Sankey, 1993).

Overall, the data from the present study confirm much of the general picture emerging from the earlier studies. However, the report highlights, because of the emphasis on pupil perspectives in the data gathering, the usefulness of listening to what pupils have to say about teaching and learning. What the present study also adds is a discussion of the significance of departmental policy and of effective classroom management strategies in shaping attitudes and raising achievement.

References for APPENDIX C

Aplin, R. (1991) 'Why do pupils opt out of foreign language courses?'. *Educational Studies,* **17,** 3–13.

APU (1985). *Foreign language performance in schools.* DES.

Arnot, M. (1982). 'Male hegemony, social class and women's education'. *Journal of Education,* **164,** 64–89.

Barton, A. (1997) 'Boys' underachievement in GCSE Modern Languages: reviewing the reasons'. *Language Learning Journal,* **16,** 11–16.

Batters, J. (1986) 'Do boys really think languages are just girl-talk?'. *Modern Languages,* **67,** 75–79.

Beswick, C. (1976) 'Mixed or single-sex for French?'. *Audio-Visual Language Journal,* **14,** 34–38.

Bugel, K. and Buunk, B. P. (1996) 'Sex differences in foreign language text comprehension: the role of interests and prior knowledge'. *Modern Languages Journal,* **80,** 15–28.

Burstall, C. Jamieson, M., Cohen, S. and Hargreaves, M. (1974) *Primary French in the balance.* NFER.

Cheng, Y., Payne, J. and Witherspoon, S. (1995). *Science and Mathematics in full-time education after 16.* Youth Cohort Report No. 36. DfEE.

Clark, A. and Trafford, J. (1994*) A study of the effect of gender on pupil attitudes and performance.* University of Sheffield.

Clark, A. and Trafford, J. (1995) 'Boys into Modern Languages: an investigation of the discrepancy in attitudes and performance between boys and girls in Modern Languages'. *Gender and Education,* **7,** 315–25.

Clark, A. and Trafford, J. (1996). 'Return to gender: boys' and girls' attitudes and achievements'. *Language Learning Journal,* **14,** 40–49.

Dickinson, L. (1995). 'Autonomy and motivation: A literature review'. *System,* **23,** 165–174.

Downes, P. (1998). 'Languages could be the key to those lost boys'. *Times Educational Supplement,* 10 April.

Graham, S. and Rees, F. (1995). 'Gender differences in language learning: the question of control'. *Language Learning Journal,* **11,** 18–19.

Halliwell, S. and Jones, B. (1991) *On target: teaching in the target language.* CILT

Harris, V. (1998) 'Making boys make progress'. *Language Learning Journal,* **18,** 56–62.

Jackson, P. and Lahadenne, H. (1971). *Inequalities of teacher–pupil contacts.* In: Melvin, Klainin, S., Fensham, P. and West, L. (1989*).* 'The superior achievement of girls in Chemistry and Physics in upper secondary schools in Thailand'. *Research and Science Technological Education, 7,* 5–14.

Lee, J., Buckland, D. and Shaw, G. (1998*) The invisible child: the responses and attitudes to the learning of Modern Foreign Languages shown by Year 9 pupils of average ability.* A report of a joint research project carried out by CILT and Barking and Dagenham LEA. CILT.

Locke, J. (1989). *Some thoughts concerning education.* Yolton J. S. and Yolton J.W. Clarendon Press. First published 1693.

Loulidi, R. (1990). 'Is language learning really a female business?' *Language Learning Journal,* Spring, 40–43.

Mifsud, C. (1993) 'Gender differentials in the classroom'. *Research in Education, 49,* 11–12.

Moore, J. (1996). 'Boys and the soft stuff'. *All-in Success, 7,* 22–23.

OFSTED (1993) *Boys and English.* HMSO.

Ormerod, M.B. (1975). 'Subject preference and choice in co-educational and single-sex secondary schools'. *British Journal of Educational Psychology, 45,* 262.

Philips, D. and Filmer-Sankey, C. (1993*). Diversification in Modern Languages teaching.* Routledge.

Place, D. J. (1997). 'Boys will be boys': boys and underachievement in MFL. *Language Learning Journal, 16,* 3–10.

Politzer, R.L. (1983) 'An exploratory study of self-reported language learning behaviours and their relation to achievement'. *Studies in Second Language Acquisition, 6,* 54–68.

Powell, R. (1979) 'Sex differences and language learning: a review of the evidence'. *Audio-Visual Language Journal, 17,* 19–24.

Powell, R. (1986). *Boys, girls and languages in school.* CILT.

Powell, R. and Batters, J. (1985). 'Pupils' perceptions of foreign language learning at 12+: some gender differences'. *Educational Studies, 11,* 11–23.

Powell, B. and Batters, J. (1986). 'Sex of teacher and the image of foreign languages in schools'. *Educational Studies, 12,* 245–254.

Powell, B. and Littlewood, P. (1982) 'Foreign languages: the avoidable options'. *British Journal of Language Teaching, 20,* 153–159.

Pritchard, R. (1987) 'Boys' and girls' attitudes towards French and German'. *Educational Research, 29,* 69.

QCA (1998) *Can do better: raising boys' achievement in English.* QCA Publications.

Reynolds, R. (1995). 'Boys and English: so what's the problem?' *The English and Media Magazine, 33,* 15–18.

Riddell, S. (1992) *Gender and the politics of the curriculum.* Routledge.

Sammons, P. (1995) 'Gender, ethnic and socio-economic differences in attainment and progress: a longitudinal analysis of student achievement over 9 years'. *British Educational Research Journal, 21,* 465–485.

Spender, D. (1982) *Invisible women: the schooling scandal.* Writers and Readers.

Stables, A. and Stables, S. (1996) 'Modern languages at A level: the danger of curricular discontinuity'. *Language Learning Journal,* **14,** 50–2.

Syal, R. and Trump, S. (1996). 'Single-sex classes raise boys' grades'. *The Sunday Times,* 25 August.

Tannen, D. (1995) *Talking from 9 to 5.* Virago Press.

Trudgill, P. (1974) *Sociolinguistics: an introduction.* Penguin.

Warrington, M. and Younger, M. (1996). 'Goals, expectations and motivation: gender differences in achievement at GCSE, *Curriculum,* **17,** 80–93.

Wheatley, J. (1996) 'Outclassed'. *The Times Magazine,* 30 March, 17–20.

Whitehead, F., Capey, A.C., Maddren, W. and Wellings, A. (1977*) Children and their books.* Macmillan Educational.

Wilkinson, L.C. and Marrett, C.B. (eds.) (1985) *Gender influences in classroom interaction.* Academic Press.